The Politics of Cri...

The Politics of Childhood

by

Martin Hoyles

and

Phil Evans

Journeyman

First published by the Journeyman Press Ltd 1989

The Journeyman Press Limited, 97 Ferme Park Road
Crouch End, London N8 9SA and
Journeyman/Kampmann & Company, 226 West 26th Street
New York, NY 10001

Copyright © 1989 by Martin Hoyles and Phil Evans

All rights reserved. No part of this publication may be
reproduced, stored in a retrieval system, opr transmitted, in any
form or by any means, electronic, mechanical, photocopying,
recording or otherwise, without the prior permission of the
publisher.

British Library Cataloguing in Publication Data

Hoyles, Martin
 The politics of childhood.
 1. Childhood
 I. Title   II. Evans, Phil
305.2'3

ISBN 1-85172-011-1

Picture research and illustrations by Phil Evans

First edition 1989

10 9 8 7 6 5 4 3 2 1

Computer typeset from disc in 11/13 Times, and
printed in Great Britain by Richard Clay Ltd, Suffolk

For Celia
with love, Martin

Contents

Chapter One

THE MYTH OF CHILDHOOD

Children should be seen and not heard
The happiest days of your life
Not in front of the children
He's too little to understand
Isn't she sweet
He's throwing another tantrum
You're only young once
Children playing at politics
Ask your parents' permission
Go out and play

Do as you're told
Do as I say
Behave yourselves
Stand up straight
Take your hands out of your pockets
Line up quietly
Look at me when I'm speaking to you
Shut up and sit down

Our present myth of childhood portrays children as not being political or sexual, as depending wholly on adults, and never engaged in serious activities such as work or culture. It is typified at Christmas by the image of the babe in the manger who grows into gentle Jesus meek and mild. This is the model of childhood which has been presented to young school children all over the country. Religious Education was the only compulsory school subject until the 1988 Act laid down the core curriculum. Nothing strange is seen in the picture of a five-year-old child, with hands clasped, praying to God in school assembly. But imagine the same child standing with clenched fist upraised and immediately there would be charges of indoctrination. Children are apparently capable of religious understanding, but not political awareness. Particularly at Christmas, with the vast sale of toys, children are celebrated sentimentally as playthings. They are played with, and all they can do is play.

Clearly this is only one view of Jesus, which Blake refutes:

> Was Jesus Humble? or did he
> Give any proofs of Humility?
> When but a Child he ran away
> And left his Parents in dismay.

It is crucial to look at different interpretations of childhood historically, to see that childhood is a social construction and not just a natural state.

Playtime at an East End school

1545 - First English book on pediatrics (treatment of children's diseases) published

1558 - First recorded doll's house, made for the daughter of Duke Albrecht of Saxony

1657 - First picture book for children 'Orbis Pictus' (The World in Pictures), compiled by Comenius, Moravian bishop and educationalist

1692 - First adaptation for children of Aesop's Fables

1744 - First English book of nursery rhymes, 'Tommy Thumb's Pretty Song Book'

1750 - First toy shops in London

1759 - First English educational board game with dice

1762 - First jigsaw puzzle, showing a map to teach geography

1851 - Montanari Dolls (forerunners of present dolls) shown at the Great Exhibition

1855 - 'Boy's Own Magazine' first published

1865 - First clockwork trains

1897 - Invention of plasticine

In Europe the cult of the Infant Jesus which symbolises childish innocence dates from the seventeenth century. Increased attention was given in religious literature and education to the holy childhood of Jesus. One of the most common devotional prints in Europe was of Christ summoning the little children to his knee. Increasingly the child became a special creature with a different nature and needs, requiring separation and protection from the adult world.

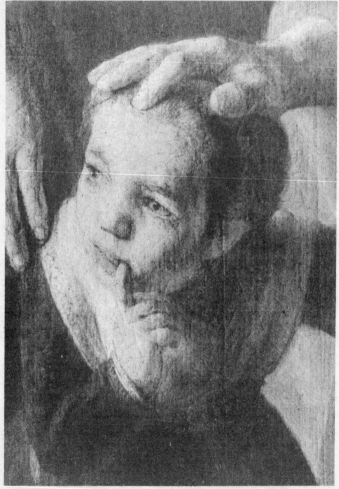

'Christ Blessing Children': School of Rembrandt c.1660

This construction of childhood as a completely separate state begins in the towns with the change from feudalism to capitalism. It is accompanied by the growth of schooling. *The first modern children were middle class and male*. Girls could learn their future work at home and so did not need to go to school.

Similarly it is clear from the way working-class children had to work in the mines, potteries and mills that there was no childhood for them. On the land too, as the philosopher **John Locke** observed in 1697, the children of the poor had to work for some part of the day from the age of three. **Mrs Burrows** recalls this aspect of country childhood in the 1850s:

> On the day that I was eight years of age, I left school, and began
> to work fourteen hours a day in the fields, with from forty to fifty
> other children of whom, even at that early age, I was the eldest.
> We were followed all day long by an old man carrying a long whip
> in his hand which he did not forget to use. A great many of the
> children were only five years of age.

The rising middle classes wanted their sons educated in a particular way to prepare them for their adult jobs and to challenge the power of the aristocracy. This led to the development of schooling and the modern concept of childhood. As early as the fourteenth century you can see the beginnings of the English and Maths based curriculum. For a career as a merchant a boy had to learn to read and do accounting before being apprenticed in a bank or a shop. For instance, a member of the Valori family of Florence, born in 1354, writes:

> In 1363, when the plague stopped, I Bartolomeo, was put to learn
> grammar at the school of Master Manovello and I stayed there up
> to 1367 through the month of May. And then in June of the same
> year I was put to learn the abacus to know how to keep accounts ,
> with Master Tomaso, and I stayed there up to February, 1368.
> And on the same day I was sent to the bank of Bernardo.

In the fifteenth century an increasing number of people wanted their sons 'put to school', especially fathers who were of the gentry or yeoman class. And in the sixteenth and seventeenth centuries there was an unparalleled middle-class investment in education.

For anyone wishing to enter one of the professions, an education at a grammar school was customary. The middle classes poured their wealth into endowment of education between 1560 and 1660 probably to a greater extent relatively than during any other hundred years in English history. Not that their offspring always appreciated it! Shakespeare lived during this period and describes

> the whining school-boy, with his satchel,
> And shining morning face, creeping like snail
> Unwillingly to school.

The construction of this new kind of life for a certain group of children was the basis on which the new myth of childhood was to be built. Now in the twentieth century, in the west, it is difficult to look at children and avoid the power of the myth as it has been developed. It is presented in media images and it is set in the structures which control children's lives, such as the school and the family. One way of deconstructing the myth is to analyse its history (chapter two) and show how it has been built up over the centuries. Another is to look at other cultures (chapter three) and see an alternative status for children. A third way (constituting the rest of the book) is to demonstrate the way that the myth is challenged by children's own words and actions, particularly in the key areas of work, sexuality and politics.

Chapter Two

THE HISTORICAL PERSPECTIVE

The new borne babe is full of the stains and pollutions of sin which it inherits from our first parents through our loins. **Richard Allestree**, 1658

The modern reader of the diary in which Henri IV's physician, Heroard, recorded the details of the young Louis XIII's life is astonished by the liberties which people took with children, by the coarseness of the jokes they made, and by the indecency of gestures made in public which shocked nobody and which were regarded as perfectly natural. No other document can give us a better idea of the non-existence of the modern idea of childhood at the beginning of the seventeenth century. **Philippe Ariès**

How has childhood changed over the centuries? In Europe in the Middle Ages children were dressed exactly like adults. As soon as they were out of swaddling bands they adopted the dress of their parents. This was the case up until the seventeenth century. Differences in dress signified class differences, not those of age. Sex wasn't differentiated either, until the age of five. Boys were dressed just like girls up to that age.

Girl, aged 20 months, wearing a gown unmatching sleeves, probably detachable under the wings. Apron with bib and matching falling band, i.e. turn-down collar. On her head a coif under a small Mary Stuart hood. She holds a rattle with bells and coral tip. 1572.

Boy aged 6 months in long gown and apron. Winged sleeves, tall bonnet. He holds a rattle with bells and tipped with a stick of coral. 1564.

Similarly there was no division between games played by adults and those played by children of the same class. Adults played hide and seek and blind man's buff and had snowball fights. The whole community took part in religious festivals, singing, dancing and performing plays.

Adults and children share games on the frozen Thames, 17th Century

In **Heroard's** diary about **Louis XIII**, at the beginning of the seventeenth century, we can see how the young prince participated in the same activities as the adults of his class. When he was three he was dancing adult dances and taking part in court ballets. Aged five he was watching bear-baiting, badger racing and practising archery. At the age of six he played chess and charades, at seven went to see comedies and started to ride and hunt. He took part in raffles, played tennis and hockey, sang, and played the violin and lute. He watched wrestling matches, jousting and bull-fighting.

Nowadays adults usually avoid reference to sexual matters in the presence of young children. This notion was entirely foreign to the society of old, as **Philippe Ariès**, the French historian, illustrates by referring to an early seventeenth century painting of a Circumcision scene:

> The scene of the Circumcision is surrounded by a crowd of children, some of them with their parents, others climbing the pillars to get a better view. For us, surely there is something strange, almost shocking, about the choice of the Circumcision as a festival of childhood, depicted in the midst of children. Shocking for us, perhaps, but not for a present-day Muslim or for a man of the sixteenth or early seventeenth century.

The Christian religion taught that children were born with an inheritance of sin and wickedness so they were in the same danger of hell as adults. They were treated as little adults and subjected to the same religious pressures, disciplines and experiences as adults. Puritan literature was full of children's religious experiences. For example, a girl between eight and nine years of age 'spent a large part of the night in weeping and praying, and could scarce take any rest day or night for some time together, desiring with all her soul to escape from the everlasting flames.'

Children mixed with adults in everyday life: they worked together. Education was carried out by means of apprenticeship. Children were not kept at home. They were sent to another house, to live and start their life there, or to learn the good manners of a knight, or a trade, or even to go to school and learn Latin.

This form of apprenticeship was common to all classes in society. The system of putting out children was commented on by an Italian in the fifteenth century:

> The want of affection in the English is strongly manifested towards their children; for after having kept them at home till they arrive at the age of seven or nine years at the utmost, they put them out, both males and females, to hard service in the houses of other people, binding them generally for another seven or nine years. And these are called apprentices, and during that time they perform all the most menial offices; and few are born who are exempted from this fate, for everyone, however rich he may be, sends his children into the houses of others, whilst he, in return, receives those of strangers into his own.

Work was something that you started early and learnt on the job. **Daniel Defoe** said in 1724 that all children over the age of four or five could earn their own bread. Apprenticeship was compulsory after the age of twelve and some began as young as seven. Children of eleven joined the army and you could be a lieutenant by the age of fourteen.

Education could spread over the whole span of human life, without giving special value to childhood. You could start school at ten years old or at twenty. In the fifteenth century instruction was given in the same room to several hundred children of all different ages. Eton in 1517 had only one school room, and in France as late as the seventeenth century you could find a twenty four year old man in the same class as an eleven year old child. Twelve year olds went to Oxford and Cambridge, though by the seventeenth century the age of entry was usually fifteen.

Levels of education were not attached to different ages, so there are many examples of what we would consider precocious behaviour. **Melancthon** wrote a comedy at the age of thirteen, qualified as a bachelor at fourteen and as a doctor at seventeen. **John Evelyn's** son **Richard** by the time he was two and a half years old could not merely read English, but Latin, French and Gothic as well, speaking the first three exactly. By the time he was five he had a 'strange passion for Greeke'.

Daniel Defoe (1663-1731) and John Evelyn (1620-1706)

At the same time Tudor criminal law said you could be hanged for theft at the age of seven, and this continued up until the eighteenth century. In fact there are cases of children younger than seven being executed, such as the child of six who cried for his mother on the scaffold. In the eighteenth century nine out of ten people who were hanged were under the age of 21.

A public execution,
an occasion for all the family!

When we think of the family the setting is usually inside a house, with the family at home, but up until the sixteenth century there were hardly any interior scenes in painting. Life up until the seventeenth century was lived in public. Even the house was a public place. Nobody was ever left alone. Rooms opened on to each other; they were not separated by corridors. There were no specialist rooms. In the same rooms where they ate, people slept, danced, worked and received visitors. Beds were collapsible and any number could be set up in one room.

Children were not central to the family. Childhood was simply an unimportant phase, and the high rate of infant mortality meant that people could not allow themselves to become too attached to something that was regarded as a probable loss. You had several children in order to keep a few. Even in the eighteenth century the figures show that 75% of all children christened were dead before the age of five. And in the nineteenth century half the children born died in the first five years.

Many of the changes in these areas started to take place as early as the fifteenth century and some of them did not fully come into effect until the nineteenth century.

You find the beginning of specialisation in boys' dress in the late sixteenth century and early seventeenth century and it is connected

*'The "old" childhood of Prince Baltasar Carlos': Velazquez,
17th Century*

with the extension of schooling. There were very few schools for girls and they were still dressed as women. This specialised dress for boys occurred in middle class and aristocratic families.

Most nursery rhymes were not in the first place composed for children, certainly not those composed before the eighteenth century. But in the eighteenth century there was the beginning of a market for children's literature. **John Newbery** in 1744 was the first man to make publication of books for children a special line of business and he had help from **Oliver Goldsmith** in writing some of them.

Games began to be differentiated — some games were played only by children and others by adults.

BLIND-MAN'S BUFF.

The attitude to sex changed. This was partly due to the church, for certain religious teachers refused any longer to allow children to be given books considered indecent. The idea was born of providing censored editions of the classics for children. In England **Thomas** and **Harriet Bowdler** published *The Family Shakespeare* in 1807, from which they had removed "everything that can raise a blush on the cheek of modesty". **Charles** and **Mary Lamb** brought out their *Tales from Shakespeare* with a similar intention.

In France the Jesuits wrote new rules for administering corporal punishment. It was laid down that the trousers of the victim were not to be removed; just enough of the skin was to be exposed as was necessary to inflict the punishment, but not more!

In the seventeenth century came the beginning of the concept of childhood which stressed innocence and weakness rather than original sin. This innocence had to be preserved, the weakness protected. By the eighteenth century the French philosopher, **Rousseau**, had turned the doctrine of original sin upside down. In his book on education, *Émile* , he wanted to protect the innocent child from corruption by society.

The English poet, **William Blake**, also lived at this time, when the emerging idea of childhood innocence stood face to face with the reality of horrific child labour and very high infant mortality:

> the Cold babe
> Stands in the furious air; he cries:
> > 'the children of six thousand years
> Who died in infancy rage furious:
> > a mighty multitude rage furious,
> Naked and pale standing in the expecting air, to be deliver'd.'

Blake's *Songs of Innocence and of Experience* express this contradiction "showing the two states of the human soul", and were written specifically for children.

By the end of the eighteenth century schooling had almost eliminated apprenticeship, except in the working class. The so-called Enlightenment objected to educating the lower classes. **Voltaire**, the French philosopher, wrote:

> Thank you for condemning the education of labourers. I
> who farm the land need agricultural workers and not
> tonsured clerics. The lower classes should be guided, not
> educated: they are not worthy to be educated.

A formroom at Westminster School, 1846

Schools were for the middle classes. They made the public schools in England their preserve by the end of the eighteenth century.

The changes did not, however, affect the working class in the same way. At the beginning of this century children aged from ten to fourteen were still employed in the jute mills in Dundee from 6am to 6pm. They were an accepted part of the work force and treated as equals by the grown-ups. Social workers frowned on this practice and argued that the factory was more often than not

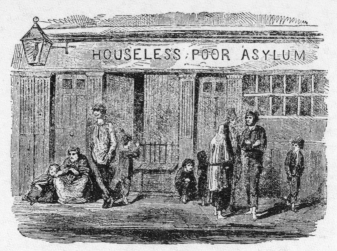

ASYLUM FOR THE HOUSELESS POOR, CRIPPLEGATE

permeated with evil influences (like loose filthy talk, gambling and drinking). The children's lives were very mixed up with the adults: the entire family often slept in a single room and the children slept where they dropped with exhaustion.

This had been a continual theme in middle-class Victorian society. They were horrified at children showing adult qualities:

> the hideous antithesis, an infant in age, a man in shrewdness and vice, the face of a child with no trace of childish goodness. **S Robins** 1851

In Ipswich in 1857 **John Glyde** saw boys gambling openly on the streets on Sundays:

> Almost all, even the boys of twelve, have acquired that habit of smoking; and obscene and disgusting language is continuously emanating from their lips.

Mary Carpenter in her *Juvenile Delinquents − Their Condition and Treatment* , written in 1853, says that young delinquents show "qualities the very reverse of what we should desire to see in childhood; we have beheld them independent, self-reliant, advanced in the knowledge of evil." She wanted them "gradually restored to the true position of childhood".

The commander of the reformatory ship *'Akbar'* saw his task in a similar light:

> The first great change which has to be affected when
> they are received on board in their vagrant state is to make
> them 'boys'. They are too old, too knowing, too sharp when
> they come on board, too much up in the ways of the world.
> (1857)

If anything demonstrates clearly the social construction of childhood, it is this attempt to 'create children':

> The delinquent is a little stunted man already - he knows
> much and a great deal too much of what is called life - he
> can take care of his own immediate interests. He is
> self-reliant, he has long directed or mis-directed his own
> actions and has so little trust in those about him, that he
> submits to no control and asks for no protection. He has
> consequently much to unlearn - he has to be turned again
> into a child.   **M D Hill** 1855

Children in schools were gradually separated according to age, and the discipline of school replaced that of apprenticeship.

In the fourteenth century students were punished by having to buy drinks or pay fines. By the sixteenth century corporal punishment had been introduced, and in the nineteenth-century

England flogging became increasingly common. It did change its meaning though, in the reform of the public schools carried out by

Thomas Arnold in the 1830s. The birch became an instrument of education, an opportunity for the boy being beaten to exercise self-control, which was the first duty of an English gentleman. The monitor or prefect could also now inflict punishment instead of just informing on other pupils.

Children were increasingly imprisoned. In the year 1847, 1,272 children under the age of 12 were sent to prison. In 1869 in Blandford, Dorset, a child of ten was imprisoned with hard labour,

---

HUNTINGDON COUNTY GAOL,

5th January 18 72

Particulars of Persons convicted of an offence specified in the First Schedule of Habitual Criminals' Act, 1869, and who will be liberated from this Gaol within seven days from date hereof, either on expiration of sentence, or on Licence from Secretary of State.

Name and Aliases   *Julia Oisgothorpe*

Photograph of Prisoner.

Description when liberated.		
Age (on discharge)	*11*	
Height	*4ft 1*	
Hair	*L Brown*	
Eyes	*Grey*	
Complexion	*Fresh*	
Where born	*Nottingham*	
Married or single		
Trade or occupation	—	
Any other distinguishing mark		

Address at time of apprehension   *Grantham*

Whether summarily disposed of or tried by a Jury.   *Summarily*

'Summarily disposed': 11-year-old Julia's criminal record of 1872

followed by five years at a reformatory school, for taking 'three pennyworth of turnips from a heap in a field'.

In 1880 the Home Secretary, **Sir William Harcourt,** told **Queen Victoria** about children being imprisoned for minor offences:

> a boy of nine years old for throwing stones; several boys of eleven and twelve years for damaging grass by running about in the fields; a girl of thirteen for being drunk; several boys of twelve and thirteen for bathing in a canal, and similarly for playing pitch and toss. Sir William humbly begs leave to represent to your Majesty that protracted imprisonment in such cases has an injurious effect both upon the physical and moral nature of the children of tender years.

The Queen replied:

> HM was really interested in all you said about the youthful criminals. She would like to whip them, but it seems that it cannot be done.

Capital punishment for children was eventually stopped in the nineteenth century although it was still on the statute book in the early part of that century. Between 1801 and 1836, 103 children under the age of fourteen received capital sentences at the Old Bailey, but they were all commuted to transportation or imprisonment.

Army methods influenced education, like the whistle, lining up in columns, solitary confinement, uniform. This type of discipline led to the rebellions which took place in French schools in the seventeenth century. They took the form of strikes, picketing, sometimes even armed riots. In eighteenth-century England the situation was the same. At Winchester the boys occupied the school for two days and hoisted the red flag. In 1818 two companies of troops with fixed bayonets had to be called in to suppress a rising of the pupils. At Rugby the pupils set fire to their books and desks and withdrew to an island which had to be taken by assault by the army. In Eton in 1783 there was a revolt against the headmaster, with rooms pillaged and windows broken. The last important revolt occurred at Marlborough as late as 1851. At Eton there were none after 1832, when the last one ended with the flogging of eighty boys.

'Grace before Meat': Jan Steen, 17th Century

In the seventeenth century there was a flood of paintings of families and interior scenes. There was a move indoors towards the intimacy of private life. By the eighteenth century the inside of the house had changed. Rooms had become independent, opening on to a corridor. There was a specialisation of rooms. No longer were beds to be found all over the house; they were confined to bedrooms. Servants now lived in separate quarters and were summoned by bells from a distance. It was no longer acceptable to call on a friend at any time of the day and without warning. Either one had days when one was 'at home', or else people sent one another cards by their servants. Increasingly a need was felt amongst the middle classes to respect each other's privacy.

What were the needs and aims of the new middle classes, the merchants, scientists and artisans who were challenging the old world, the Puritans who made the English Revolution in the seventeenth century?

Education was crucial to their advance. In the eighty years before 1640, from being a backward country in science, England became one of the most advanced. The science of Elizabeth's reign was the work of merchants and craftsmen, not academics, and was centred in London, not Oxford and Cambridge.

In feudal society, king, nobleman and peasant could all be illiterate, as **William the Conqueror** was. In the growing capitalist society literacy and numeracy were essential to understand and contribute to the scientific revolution which was taking place, and to develop trade and commerce. This is why schools like Merchant Taylors' were founded and supervised by merchant companies in the sixteenth century, Gresham College in the seventeenth, and later the Dissenting Academies. Eighteenth-century schools advertised their curriculum to appeal to the new middle classes.

Boys at Eton, 1930s

Top of the list were commercial subjects for the boys (navigation, fortification, trigonometry, surveying, merchants' accounts, foreign languages), and social graces for the girls (music, art, dancing, deportment). Consequently the sons of the middle classes were the first modern children, separated off from working activities and sent to school to undergo a long training in preparation for their adult working lives. This has led to the separation of education and work which is with us today.

Chapter Three

CROSS-CULTURAL PERSPECTIVES

Every single statement that an anthroplogist makes is a comparative statement. 'The baby is weaned at a year' compares this people to others who wean at six months, nine months, two years, at walking, when the mother is pregnant again, or who attempt never to wean the youngest child at all. **Margaret Mead**

I found three tribes all conveniently within a hundred mile area. In one, both men and women act as we expect women to act — in a mild parental repsonsive way; in the second, both act as we expect men to act — in a fierce initiating fashion; and in the third, the men act according to our stereotype for women — are catty, wear curls and go shopping, while the women are energetic, managerial, unadorned partners. **Margaret Mead**

A nthropological studies illustrate different possibilities for childhood. Margaret Mead's study of the Manus tribe of New Guinea, for example, shows a different pattern of child-rearing. After the child's first year the father begins to look after it and he expects his wife to go to work. When a new baby is born the first child is almost completely dependent on the father: he feeds it, bathes it, plays with it all day. At night the child sleeps with the father. Young children are encouraged to swim, climb, handle fire, paddle a canoe, judge distances and calculate the strength of materials. Three year olds are given tiny canoes and miniature fish spears with which they learn to spear minnows.

In northern Ghana the Tallensi also have a different attitude to children. Conversation or actions are not inhibited because children are present. The Tallensi are not surprised at the comprehensive and accurate sexual knowledge of a six year old, though no direct sexual instruction is given. Masturbation is not forbidden and there are no transition rites. When there is dancing at a homestead the children of about six years and upwards from the whole neighbourhood meet there and remain until dawn. They might tell their parents where they are going, but would not be sent for to come home.

Alternative gender roles are revealed. In the Kgatla tribe in South Africa the women do most of the productive work while the men have no regular daily work. Among the people of Bamenda the women carry all the heavy loads because they are said to have stronger foreheads than men. A group of men were heard commenting on another man: "He works hard, indeed he works almost as hard as a woman."

Transporting bananas, Rewa river, Fiji

Among the Mbuti in Africa both sexes take part in hunting and gathering. They also share political decisions and have the same social status. There is very little division of labour by sex. Men often care for even the youngest children. The Mbuti language distinguishes between the sexes only in terms of parenthood. They have words for mother and father, but not for girl and boy, woman and man.

People living in the Brazilian highlands do not emphasise temperamental differences between the sexes. Boys and girls show the same good-humoured sexual aggressiveness. The term for intercourse may have a masculine or a feminine object. Among the Zuni Indians the association of sexual aggressiveness with femininity means that the male, and not the female, faces the wedding night with fear and trembling.

In a Southwest Pacific society it is only the men who wear flowers in their hair and scented leaves tucked into their belts or arm-bands. At formal dances it is the man who dresses in the most elegant finery. When the young men are fully made up and costumed for the dance they are considered so irresistible to women that they are not allowed to be alone, even for a moment, for fear some woman will seduce them.

Instead of using these insights into the cultural construction of childhood, the child-study industry has based its research largely on psychology which concentrates on the child as an individual, is usually ethnocentric, and ignores the political context of childhood.

Why is there so much research into the differences between children and adults? Clearly it is a political choice. Similarly with the debate on the differences between male and female, or black and white. In effect it justifies and perpetuates the present split between adults and children.

Chapter Four

EXCLUSION FROM WORK

We have, Sir, this night made one of the greatest
discoveries ever made by a House of Commons, a discovery
which will be hailed by the constituents of the Hon.
Gentlemen behind me with singular pleasure. Hitherto, we
have been told that our navy was the glory of the country,
and that our maritime commerce and extensive
manufactures were the mainstay of the realm. We have also
been told that the land has its share in our greatness, and
should justly be considered as the pride and glory of
England. The Bank, also, has put in its claim to share in this
praise, and has stated that public credit is due to it; but now,
a most startling discovery has been made, namely, that all
our greatness and prosperity, that our superiority over other
nations, is owing to 300,000 little girls in Lancashire. We
have made the notable discovery that, if these little girls
work two hours less in a day than they do now, it would
occasion the ruin of the country; that it would enable other
nations to compete with us; and thus make an end to our
boasted wealth, and bring us to beggary! **William Cobbett**
(Speech in the House of Commons, 18 July 1833)

I wish the school was like a job. You could do your work
and if it is good you get money for it. **Ten year old girl**

I don't like adults because they won't let you do jobs like
paper rounds. My dad says, 'Yeah, you can do it but ask
your mum first.' When I ask she says, 'No you're too young
to be doing all that yet! **Ten year old boy**

According to a report published by the Low Pay Unit in
1985 two out of every five eleven to sixteen year olds
have a part-time job in term time, four fifths of them
illegally. More than half of the total earned £1 an hour and one
fifth earned less than 50p an hour. The majority worked for ten

hours or less a week, but a few did a full-time job as well as school work. One London boy worked 36 hours a week for about 17p an hour.

Despite these findings, children over the past century have gradually been separated from the adult world of work. Before the industrial revolution most work was done in or around the home and the household was an economic unit.

At the beginning of the nineteenth century, despite the hard work done by children, there was still the possibility of them feeling a sense of responsibility and pride in their contribution to the family income, as a number of working class autobiographies show:

> I was born in 1836 in Daventry, Northamptonshire, of very
> Poor Parents. My Father was a Tailor by Trade and my
> Mother assisted him in his work. Times were very Bad and
> they found it hard to Live. At the age of six I remember my
> Father working in a Garrett where I Slept, until ten o'clock
> at night. At the age of eight I went to work in the Fields,
> scaring Birds for seven days a week at a wage of one shilling.
> This sum Bought my Mother a four Pound Loaf. **James
> Hawker**

Birdscaring: Charles Keenes

The son of a Somerset farm-labourer, at the age of ten, earned threepence a day as a cowkeeper:

> Small as the sum was, however, I knew it would be very
> acceptable to my persevering father and mother who were toiling
> early and late to supply our wants; and the munificent payment
> was accordingly accepted. **Henry White**

Girls' work was also necessary to supplement the family income. Straw plaiting (to make straw hats) was begun at the age of three or four. One girl recalls how she had her first lesson when only three years old. She was given three or four splints of straw and was taught how to twist them under and over to the words and tune of a little song, "Under one and over two, Pull it tight and that will do". By the age of four "she had become so advanced in the art that she was able to earn 1s.6d. per week by plaiting". In Lancashire very young children were employed picking shrimps:

> You may see in many houses mere infants seated at a
> table and thus employed for hours together. The shrimps are
> prepared for potting or tea parties, and children 4 years old
> can earn in this way 6d. or 9d. a day.

As the factory system spread, it destroyed the economic unit of the household. Work became split from family life, so threatening its disruption.

The early working class defended child labour, as it preserved the traditional ties between children and their parents, particularly their fathers who taught them a skill. But with the spread of the factory system when every worker (man, woman and child) became a similar cog in the industrial machine, men's authority over women and parents' authority over children were both threatened. Men were often put out of work by women and children who could be employed at less than half the wages.

Frederick Engels refers to this, at the same time attacking "the collecting of persons of both sexes and all ages in a single work-room". He quotes a speech made by **Lord Ashley** in the House of Commons, 15th March 1844:

> A man berated his two daughters for going to the
> public-house, and they answered that they were tired of
> being ordered about, saying, 'Damn you, we have to keep
> you!' Determined to keep the proceeds of their work for
> themselves, they left the family dwelling, and abandoned
> their parents to their fate.

In the same period **John Doherty,** mule-spinner and radical trade unionist, expressed similar worries about children's sexual and financial independence and their growing power and authority:

> For everyone will admit, that to place persons of both
> sexes, of fifteen or sixteen years, indiscriminately together,
> and put them in receipt of 12s and 16s a week, which is
> entirely at their own disposal, without education and before
> their habits are fixed, and their reason sufficiently mature to
> control their passions and restrain their appetites, such
> persons will not grow up as chaste, moral and obedient, as if
> they had still remained under the salutary restraint of
> parental control. If the practice were to become general, of
> employing girls and boys instead of men, it could place the
> son and daughter of fifteen, at the head of the family, to
> whose whims and caprices the father must bend and
> succumb, or in many cases starve.

Opposition to girls working was based particularly on the view of femininity put forward by middle class men. Girls were meant to grow up into weak, dependent, modest women who would make 'good' wives and mothers. This is why the various reports of the Commissioners on the Employment of Children in the 1860s attacked the work of girls in agriculture, because field work encouraged "strong passions, rough language and general loudness" in children. Straw plaiting was condemned:

> The great want of chastity amongst the plait girls
> probably arises from the early age at which the girls become
> independent of their parents, and often leave their homes,
> and from the fact that male and female plaiters go about the
> lanes together in summer engaged in work which has not
> even the wholesome corrective of more or less physical
> exhaustion.

Similarly the morality of girls making gloves was criticised and their independence deplored:

> At an early age they become independent of their parents
> and submit to no control, even when it is exercised
> judiciously. The evil-disposed at once go out to lodge, if
> their parents will not allow them to keep late hours; their
> morality is very low, their ignorance excessive, and their
> language and behaviour often very rough and coarse.

The one area of girls' work which was not investigated by the Commissioners was that of 'service'. More girls were employed as servants than in any other occupation, but this was acceptable as they were supposed to be learning manners and their future role in life as wives and mothers.

Servants' work, a preparation for
marriage and motherhood

At the beginning of this century a section of the working class was still opposed to ending child labour for an economic reason. The 1902 Trades Union Congress carried the Gasworkers' Union resolution to prohibit the employment of children under fifteen years of age by only 535,000 to 514,000 votes. As **Jack London** commented:

> When 514,000 workers oppose a resolution prohibiting child-labour under fifteen, it is evident that a less-than-living wage is being paid to an immense number of the adult workers of the country.

Nevertheless it was opposition to this exploitation of child labour which created the movement to remove children from the factories and the land, and to put them into schools till fourteen, fifteen, and now sixteen years of age. It is understandable when you read the reports on the working conditions of children, for instance the eight-year-old girl employed in a mine for thirteen hours a day, opening and closing traps:

> I have to trap without a light and I'm scared. Sometimes
> I sing when I've a light, but not in the dark; I dare not sing
> then.

A child's rope harness, c.1840

Another eight-year-old girl worked in a mill from five in the morning until nine at night:

> I sometimes should have slept as I walked if I had not
> stumbled and started awake again; and so sick often that I
> could not eat, and what I did eat I vomited.

In the manufacture of glass, the hard labour, the irregularity of the hours, the frequent night-work, and especially the great heat of the working place (100 to 130 Fahrenheit) engender in children general debility and disease, stunted growth, and especially affections of the eye, bowel complaint, and rheumatic and bronchial affections. Many of the children are pale, have red eyes, often blind for weeks at a time, suffer from violent nausea, vomiting, coughs, colds and rheumatism. When the glass is withdrawn from the fire, the children must often go into such heat that the boards on which they stand catch fire under their feet. The glassblowers usually die young of debility and chest affections. **Frederick Engels**

But if work were democratically organised in our society, why should children not work?

It is obvious that the collective working group of individuals of both sexes and all ages must under the appropriate conditions turn into a source of humane development, although in its spontaneously developed, brutal, capitalist form, the system works in the opposite direction, and becomes a pestiferous source of corruption and slavery, since here the worker exists for the process of production, and not the process of production for the worker. **Karl Marx**

Marx and Engels make it clear in the *Manifesto of the Communist Party* that it is not children's work as such that they wish to abolish. The tenth demand reads: "Free education for all children in public schools. Abolition of children's factory labour *in its present form.* Combination of education with industrial production."

Marx develops the idea in *Capital :*

The germ of the education of the future is present in the factory system; this education will, in the case of every child over a given age, combine productive labour with instruction and gymnastics, not only as one of the methods of adding to the efficiency of production, but as the only method of producing fully developed human beings.

Similarly in 1871 the Paris Commune's Education Commission claimed the "right to a complete education and training corresponding to the inclination and abilities of each individual and enabling him actually to begin working in his chosen occupation."

Charles Fourier, the French utopian who influenced Marx, describes in detail a whole production process which is to be carried out by very young children:

> We will take as an example a little task which can be performed by the youngest children - the shelling and sorting of green peas. In civilised society this task occupies thirty-year-old persons. In Harmony it will be assigned to children of two, three and four years. Their task is to separate the smallest peas for sweet stew, the medium peas for a stew made with bacon, and the large peas for soup.

In China primary school children do short periods of productive work, like sorting grain or making boxes. In one school they make

Our little factory: painting by 13-year-old Chinese pupil

the metal handrails for the boarding platforms of buses and the metal edges of the steps. So every bus they see in the street is proof of their work.

In Budapest there is a narrow gauge railway thirteen miles long overlooking the Danube, which is staffed, with the exception of the engine driver, by ten to fifteen year old members of the Young Pioneers. They come from local schools and take it in turn to perform the functions of ticket clerks, conductors, telegraphers and signal operators. The Pioneer Railway was set up in 1952, in imitation of those in the Soviet Union, and has run ever since without any mishaps.

Guard on the Pioneer Railway, Budapest

Children also demonstrate their maturity and responsibility in cultural and social spheres. The Japanese music teacher **Suzuki** has shown how 'average' five year olds can learn to play the violin with amazing skill without devoting the whole of their lives to it.

An example of a baby comforting her distressed mother is recorded by an American social worker, **Elizabeth Davoren**:

> I remember watching an eighteen-month-old soothe her mother, who was in a state of high anxiety and tears. First she put down the bottle she was sucking. Then she moved about in such a way

that she could approach, then touch, and eventually calm her mother down (something I had not been able to do). When she sensed her mother was comfortable again, she walked across the floor, lay down, picked up her bottle, and started sucking it again.

You only have to look at children in advertisements or read children's books, to see the image of childhood that is presented by adults in this country. Compare a couple of books from China. *Little Sisters of the Grassland* is the story of two Mongolian girls, aged nine and eleven, who battle through a blizzard for a whole day and night to protect their flock of sheep. And in *Secret Bulletin* a boy and girl before the revolution are involved in printing and distributing revolutionary bulletins. Significantly it is the girl who takes the initiative, she knows more about how to print the bulletins than the boy, she thinks quickly to save him getting caught and she gets beaten in order to protect him.

When a class of six year olds in a London infant school were asked to draw pictures of adults and children, they drew the following activities:

ADULTS	CHILDREN
Painting	Jumping up and down
Climbing a ladder	Pulling a toy bus
Chopping up wood	Playing badminton
Washing the floor	Playing with a car
Driving a car	Flying a kite
Driving a lorry	Kicking a football
Picking flowers	Playing cowboys and Indians
Mending a car	Watching Bugs Bunny
Cleaning windows	Skipping
Hoovering	Going to school
Chopping down trees	Playing with bricks
Cutting the grass	Reading
	Sliding down
	Drawing

The children are nearly all playing and the adults working. But the work the adults are doing is mainly domestic work, as the children are cut off from seeing the work which their parents *go out* to do.

In the evening I wait for daddy to come home
just like mommy.
I'm daddy's girl just like mommy.

I have fun just like daddy

Just Like Mommy, Just Like Daddy, *Wonder Books, 1952*

Chapter Five

THE SUPPRESSION OF SEXUALITY

Parents, sexual knowledge is immodest, impure and corrupting. May you shield the flower of innocence from such improper knowledge. **Professor D S Fowler** 1870

Far more openly sexual behaviour occurs among small children than is usually admitted. **Susan Isaacs** 1933

I have decided to be open about my sexuality. Being a lesbian means loving a person of my own sex. This is a political statement as well as a sexual one. **Allyson**, American high school student, 1976

I cannot remember a day in my life when I did not have sexual feelings. Since the dawn of my memory, not only can I remember being sexually aware but also sexually active to a certain degree. When I was five or six I first became sexually active with my playmates, but I was never the first to initiate anything. What we did seems primitive now but actually it isn't as childish as it seems. We were human beings who had no social inhibitions and were willing to explore our sexuality to its fullest extent. **Aaron Fricke** 1981

D espite Freud's work on infant sexuality, children are still seen basically as not being sexual. Again, the seventeenth century marks the beginning of this view. Children's sexuality was considered dangerous. The custom of children all sleeping together in the same bed was attacked. In schools there was a steady separation of the sexes and of age groups.

The publication in 1710 of *Onania: Or, The Heinous Sin of Self Pollution, and all its frightful Consequences in both Sexes considered with spiritual and Physical Advice to those who have* *already injur'd themselves by this abominable Practise* marked the beginning of a campaign against masturbation.   In 1800, though, we can still find an example of children's sex play being openly accepted. In that year **Harriette Wilson** visited her married sister and saw her children romping about naked. The two year old girl was playing with the penis of her four and a half year old brother. "Is Sophie to have my didoodle to keep?" he asked his mother. "No, my love," came the calm reply, "not to keep, only to play with."

Lovers: Maillol

In the nineteenth century sex was discussed more than ever, but with the purpose of strictly defining its 'normal' channels and condemning anything 'abnormal'. So homosexuality and masturbation, for example, were seen as sins or diseases.

The German philosopher **Kant** wrote in 1803:

> Nothing weakens the mind as well as the body so much as the kind
> of lust which is directed towards themselves, and it is entirely at
> variance with the nature of man. But this also must not be
> concealed from the youth. We must place it before him in all its
> horribleness, telling him that in this way he will become useless for
> the propagation of the race, that his bodily strength will be ruined
> by this vice more than by anything else, that he will bring on
> himself premature old age, and that his intellect will be very much
> weakened.

Dr **William Acton,** the (in)famous nineteenth century authority
on sex, describes the boy who masturbates:

> The frame is stunted, the muscles underdeveloped, the
> eye is sunken and heavy, the complexion is sallow, pasty or
> covered with spots of acne, the hands are damp and cold,
> and the skin moist. His intellect has become sluggish and
> enfeebled and if his evil habits are persisted in, he may end
> in becoming a drivelling idiot.

And Dr **Henry Maudsley** wrote in 1867 that masturbation
"gives rise to a particular and disagreeable form of insanity
characterized by intense self-feeling and conceit."

Storm over sex classes for under-16s at GLC's on-the-rates gay centre

In 1965 an opinion poll revealed that 93% of people saw homosexuality as a form of illness needing medical treatment. The British Social Attitudes survey, involving 1,700 people nationwide, shows that hostility to homosexuality has recently increased. In 1983, 62% thought homosexual relationships always or mostly wrong against 69% in 1986. Those saying homosexuality is not wrong at all has fallen from 17% to 13%.

In the twentieth century **Wilhelm Reich** stressed the positive side of children's sexuality, much of his writing being based on close contact with workers' youth groups in Germany and Austria. He gives an interesting account of the children's home founded in August 1921 by the Moscow psychoanalyst **Vera Schmidt**. The teachers were told there were to be no punishments, no praise or blame, no violent demonstrations of affection. Masturbation and sexual curiosity were not forbidden. Toilet training was not forced.

The authorities eventually withdrew financial support from the home. From April 1922 it was provided with food and coal by the German and Russian miners' unions. Nevertheless it was finally forced to close. Reich concludes:

> The work of Vera Schmidt was the first attempt in the history of education to give the theory of infantile sexuality a practical content. As always in the course of the sexual revolution, authorities, 'scientists', psychologists and established educators paved the way for regression and defeat, while trade unionists, without any theoretical knowledge, showed in a practical way that they had grasped the full importance of the problem.

Children at the art gallery: Gotthard Schuh

In Britain **Dora Russell** and **A S Neill** best exemplify the acknowledgement of children's sexuality at school. Neill saw Reich as "the sanest man on early ruination of children that I ever knew". At Summerhill he admitted that he could not allow a full adolescent sex life for fear the school would be closed down, but he continually argued against what he considered to be the prevailing attitude that sex is not right, that there is something wrong with it:

> This anti-sexual attitude, inculcated in the child at the preverbal stage by the suppression of masturbation and the taboo on nakedness, may never be put into words. It is all in the atmosphere.

Dora Russell ran her Beacon Hill school on similar lines:

> In 1927 it was not accepted that even young children could be allowed to be nude in each other's presence, and should not be scolded for 'playing with themselves' as masturbation was decently called. The children saw each other naked. When they queried the difference between boys and girls and, at shower times, perhaps, the boys would boast of their 'tails', we might say that possibly girls thought them funny with those things on, and anyway, girls could have babies.

Sexuality has always been a contentious issue within our family. Basically it seems to me that in my parents' eyes sex does not exist. They try to hide it and rarely talk about it. Neither of them has ever volunteered any information with regards to sex or contraception. When I was nine I asked Mum what a virgin was and she told me she did not know. At the age of eleven I got my nine year old sister to ask Mum what it felt like to fuck. Her shocked answer was not to use that disgusting word. That was the sum total of our parental sex education. **Anne Fullam**

If heterosexual relations between children are suppressed in our society, other forms of sexual relations are given the full shock-horror treatment.

The lack of reference to homosexuality in school is most striking, especially when compared with the continual propaganda for heterosexuality. In this country teachers are often frightened to deal with the issue and some teachers have been sacked for 'coming out' in school. Similarly most states in the USA have statutes in their educational codes about teachers' morals, one of the purposes being to remove homosexual school teachers. But it is the responsibility of all teachers to combat heterosexism. As with fighting racism, this involves giving up the power which comes from belonging to a dominant group, a strategy which has not begun to be developed yet. Nor have many people begun to see homosexuality as a positive choice, rather than just tolerating it.

Listen to the voices of lesbian and gay teenagers recounting how they have been treated, particularly by parents and teachers, relieved only occasionally by support and encouragement. The following quotations are from research published in 1984 by the London Gay Teenage Group, whose chairperson introduces the book:

"The research is the first of its kind, I believe, certainly in London. Its findings have confirmed the feelings that many of us had about hostility from society and the reaction we meet. Not only do we face oppression for being young in an 'age = wisdom' defined society, but we are also oppressed and suppressed for being gay. To overcome these incredible difficulties needs immense strength from the individual and the support of friends and groups. I hope then, that the report will make others more aware of what it is like to be young and lesbian or gay, whether at school, at home, or in other social situations."

"My girlfriend's parents found out about us and came round and told my mother. My mother didn't speak to me for about two months. It hasn't been the same since. She doesn't like the idea of me being a lesbian and every time we have an argument, (which is frequently), she calls me names, 'queer' and such like and says she hates me."

"They threw me out of the house and didn't speak to me for

months. My mother said that she wished that she had had a miscarriage while carrying me."

Frontispiece to The Fourth Pig*:*
Gertrude Hermes

"They wanted me to see a doctor."

"Very upset - they tried to finish it by a court injunction. I became very distant from them."

"I told my mother, but she didn't take me seriously (I was just 16 years old at the time). About a year later she became worried about my friendship with a straight woman and suggested that she was seducing me. The relationship was platonic. My mother went crazy and behaved as if I was doing her some great injustice. I had let her down. She felt that I was disgusting. My mother has now come round to a position of complete acceptance and support. Only a few months after her initial disgust she offered to pay for my girl-friend and I to spend a weekend in Paris for my 18th birthday present. My girlfriend and I always sleep together at my house and my mother wanders in and chats to us and even sometimes brings us morning tea in bed. She is happy for me, for us. She commented on how she had never known me to be so happy before."

"People, especially the boys, kept saying: 'Poof, gay black bastard'. The usual uneducated names."

"School referred me to a psychoanalyst or psychiatrist on the pretext of 'being worried about my work'!"

"My school was a church school. My lover was the Head Girl. We were very open. They expelled me!"

"When at school sex education did not touch at all upon gays. There were leaflets and books available on social problems, drugs, abortion, contraceptives, VD, but nothing for gays."

"School sex education said it was perverted, that if your glands over secrete then you're gay."

Each section of the book ends with a series of recommendations. Those for schools and Local Education Authorities are that:

*The specific problems and needs of young homosexuals at school be recognised, and every effort made to meet those needs and support those pupils. This would involve specific training at teacher training colleges.

*The formation of lesbian and gay pupils' groups be encouraged by all local education authorities.

*The relevance of homosexuality to many different subjects, English literature, history, social sciences, human geography and so on, be recognised, and the topic be incorporated accordingly, and dealt with in a positive manner.

*School libraries stock information leaflets, phone numbers and addresses of lesbian and gay groups, books about the lesbian and gay movement, as well as books about homosexuality and novels with positive lesbian or gay characters.

*Anti-homosexual attitudes, statements and literature be treated as seriously as racist or sexist ones.

*Lesbian and gay teachers be encouraged to be open about their sexuality and be supported in so doing. The formation of lesbian and gay teachers' groups should be encouraged by all local education authorities, who should work closely with such groups.

*To ensure all the above, all Local Education Authorities issue clear policy statements concerning the treatment of sexuality, and specifically homosexuality, in schools. This should relate to the curriculum and learning resources as well as the counselling/pastoral role of teachers.

A recent feminist contribution to the debate on children's sexuality comes from **Stevi Jackson** in her book *Childhood and Sexuality* , published in 1982. While making a plea for greater sexual freedom for children she realises the difficulty envisaging this within the present structure of society in which sex is so closely linked to domination:

> We can start by communicating more openly about sex and ceasing to conceal our own sexuality from young people. We must also avoid imposing our own preconceptions of femininity and masculinity upon them. We must stop encouraging boys to be tough and aggressive, and teach them to value gentleness, affection and tenderness instead...
>
> At the same time girls must not be prevented from gaining knowledge of their own bodies. They might be able to explore their own sexual potential, rather than viewing their sexuality as a gift for a loved male. They must be encouraged towards independence rather than passivity, to seek their own goals in life rather than serving men...
>
> Because we inhabit a society where sexuality is inextricably bound up with power and dominance, where the weak may be sexually exploited by the strong, where sexuality is exchanged as a commodity, true sexual freedom for children - and indeed for all of us - can only be illusory. It will remain a dream until sexuality is divested of its competitive and aggressive elements, separated from property and ownership, and no longer contributes to the subordination of women and children.

Chapter Six

POLITICAL ACTION

Women and children are always mentioned in the same breath ('Women and children to the forts!'). The special tie women have with children is recognized by everyone. I submit, however, that the nature of this bond is no more than shared oppression. And that moreover this oppression is intertwined and mutually reinforcing in such complex ways that we will be unable to speak of the liberation of women without also discussing the liberation of children, and vice versa. **Shulamith Firestone**

C hildren are not supposed to be politically active. Because they are denied work and responsibility, they are also thought to be incapable of involvement in politics.

A parallel can be drawn between the way children are viewed and attitudes to the working class. In *A Kestrel for a Knave*, written by **Barry Hines** in 1968, the headmaster makes a speech to the boys he is caning. He bemoans the lack of respect in young people today compared to the past:

They took it then, but not now, not in the day of the common man, when every boy quotes his rights, and shoots off home for his father as soon as I look at him.

Compare **Matthew Arnold's** fear of the assertion of working class power in 1869:

For a long time the strong feudal habits of subordination and deference continued to tell upon the working class. The modern spirit has now almost entirely dissolved those habits. More and more this and that man, and this and that body of men, all over the country, are beginning to assert and put in practice an Englishman's right to do what he likes: his right to march where he likes, meet where he likes, enter where he likes, hoot as he likes, threaten as he likes, smash as he likes. All this, I say, tends to anarchy.

The control of children in schools can be compared with the

control of inmates in prisons, patients in hospitals or people considered to be mad. All these groups are treated like 'children'. The comparison is brought home forcibly when you hear that the city of Omaha was dosing between 5% and 10% of its school children (that is three to six thousand) with amphetamine-type drugs specifically to make them amenable to school discipline. Similar treatment has been carried out in Britain. Treatment includes individual psychotherapy, behaviour therapy, drug therapy and - in some cases - brain surgery.

IF YOU HAVEN'T CONSIDERED HAVING BRAIN SURGERY, HERE'S WHY YOU SHOULD...

Look at people who speak to them and listen until they have finished without letting their eyes wander about the house. Until they are told to sit down, they are to stand quietly, are not to turn their backs to anyone nor interfere when their lord or lady is talking about the household. Especially are young people cautioned about their table manners: they are not to lean on the table, or fill their mouths too full or eat with their knives.   **The Babees Boke or A Lytl Reporte of How Young People Should Behave,** 1475

Comments from young teenagers

"I think childhood was the worst time of my life, and will be until I am sixteen years old, because during childhood you are under the rule of your mother and father all the time and cannot do a lot of the things you would like to do, like bringing girls home or going out late. All I get once I get in at night is 'Where have you bloody well been all night? Have you seen the time?'"

"There are many problems being a child because of the way different people treat you. One of the main problems is not being able to speak your mind to parents, teachers or any adults."

"My mum and dad were always particular in what company I kept which I think was terrible. It's rotten when it comes to your parents choosing your friends for you."

"If adults argue, nothing more is said about it, but if we argue with an adult we are said to be rude and an insolent child. If you start to cry or something, you're told you're a baby, so you try and act more grown up, and you're told that you're acting too grown up for your age."

"My dad was ill. I started to cry at home. All the pressures at school, all the work, and with the teachers nagging you all the time, I couldn't cope with it. I stayed at home and had to be doing something every two minutes to keep my mind off dad. I used to wash and dress my nan because she has severe arthritis, make her breakfast, go shopping and tidy up the house for mum. I would do other jobs like ironing all the boys' shirts. I just had to keep busy, I'd had so much time off school I was worried about being able to settle down again."

"All teachers get in a mood some days, but some are flash. Instead of waiting for an explanation and listening they send you out. Teachers should listen more. We listen to them so they should have the decency to listen to our views."

Children act politically when they resist being continually told what to do, particularly when they see it as being unreasonable. Despite some current theories about the moral development of children, it seems clear that children learn a sense of what is fair and unfair at a very early age, as Dickens claims in *Great Expectations*:

> In the little world in which children have their existence, whosoever brings them up, there is nothing so finely perceived and so finely felt as injustice.

Illustration by Edward Budogosky from Charles Dickens' account of childhood, Great Expectations

When an English headmaster accused school students of "playing at politics" he stated, "I am for children's rights - the right of a child to be a child." To which a member of the National Union of School Students replied, "That's a pretty dubious right!"

There are political contradictions, such as the white child who uses the language and institutional underpinning of racism to harass a black adult, or boys who harness society's sexism to insult and attack women. But mainly children are fighting against oppression. They are struggling to be *subjects* who think, feel and act in the world, rather than being the *objects* of study, emotion and control.

'Leila's fears, and how she conquered them': from Early Days, *1882*

> God rules the world with the fear of Hell and the promise
> of His kingdom. So must we too rule our children.

This is part of a treatise delivered in Antioch by **John Chrysostom**
in 388 AD. He goes on to say how the infant boy should not be
decked out in 'fine raiment and golden ornaments', but should
have a 'strict tutor' who will keep him from growing long hair!

In 1603 three apprentices in London were sent to jail for refusing
to cut their hair. Struggles still take place over clothes and hair-
styles, both at school and in the family:

> The uniform robbed us of any sexuality. In the winter it was
> green tweed pinafores that had no shape, with a green and
> white striped shirt. You had a pair of brown outdoor shoes
> (lace-ups) and brown indoor shoes (buckled), a tweed coat
> and brown beret. In the summer floral cotton print dresses in
> an assortment of colours, but the red one was for Sundays
> and special occasions, white socks, brown blazer, a boater
> with the silver school badge, and white gloves. We used the
> uniform as a form of rebellion. At one point there was a
> craze for bloomers. We would urge our mothers to send us
> some and then wear them so that the bottom showed
> underneath the hem of our pinafores. A ridiculous fashion,
> but the exercise, to show your knickers, was of great
> significance. **Liz Green**

When I was sixteen I dyed my hair - it was turquoise,
yellow and red. As I walked into the dining room everyone
was eating. Gregory said that I looked like a traffic light.
Dad took one look at me and told me to get out of the
house and never return. He then threw his knife and fork
down and stormed upstairs. **Anne Fullam**

Harmless and sociable activities like eating and talking often become serious crimes in the classroom:

> Day after day we were subjected to the same string of demands and exhortations: 'sit down, be quiet, open books, read, be quiet'. In addition to this there seemed an endless string of rules without reason: to have short nails, to tie one's hair up, to wear a tie, to walk down the corridor, to park one's bike in a specific place, to refrain from eating in any room but the dining-room. 'Do not dawdle' we were told, 'do not doodle'. In fact one had to ask permission to do anything, even to leave the room. The only subject which had any real meaning for me was Sociology... The teacher sat cross-legged on a desk, happily holding forth on her marital problems, her next door neighbour's problems, and the problems of people she described as being in a 'disadvantaged situation'... She was interested in any subject which children might come up with. She nearly always illustrated her answers with examples from her own experience. How much more credible and interesting this seemed!   **Lucy Sommers**

Turn to Exercise Ten of 'Human Relations' and get on with it quietly...

THERE'S EDUCATION —

—AND THEN THERE'S REAL EDUCATION

—so I said to him—get your hands off me, you filthy beast!

Children won't do what they ought
If you beat them with a rod.
Children thrive, children grow
When taught by words and not a blow.
Evil words, words unkind
Will do harm to a child's mind.
                Walther von der Vogelweide 1200 AD

The practice of beating children goes as far back as there are written records. In eighteenth century Europe, beating instruments included whips of all kinds, including the cat-o'-nine-tails, shovels, canes, iron and wooden rods, bundles of sticks, the discipline (a whip made of small chains), and special school instruments like the flapper, which had a pear-shaped end and a round hole to raise blisters. In Scotland the belt or tawse is used, a leather strap cut into three thongs at the end and administered on the palm of one hand or both hands together.

Childbeaters John Milton (1608-1675) and Samuel Pepys (1632-1703)

The poet **Milton** mercilessly beat his nephews. **Samuel Pepys** used to beat his fifteen year old maid with a broomstick and lock her up for the night in his cellar. **Beethoven** abused his pupils with a knitting needle and bit them. **John Wesley,** the founder of Methodism in the eighteenth century, still believed in the sinfulness of the child and that force should be used to control it:

> Break their wills betimes. Begin this work before they can run alone, before they can speak plain, perhaps before they can speak at all. Whatever pains it costs, break the will if you would not damn the child. Let a child from a year old be taught to fear the rod and to cry softly; from that age make him do as he is bid, if you whip him ten times running to effect it. Break his will now, and his soul shall live, and he will probably bless you to all eternity.

At Wesley's Kingswood School games and play were considered 'unworthy of a Christian child'. Only recreations such as chopping wood and digging were allowed.

Children gathering coal during the miners' strike, 1921

In the 1930s **Bill Bees**, a miner's son from Hanham in Gloucestershire, used to have to collect coal from the slag heap every morning, making him late for school:

> When you got to school you knew what you was going to get, you was going to get the cane for being late. If I wasn't in when the handbell went at nine o'clock the doors would be bolted so you couldn't sneak in after roll call. You was left to explain why you were so late. I had to tell 'im what I 'ad to do for my mother, but he didn't believe me, and he would get the cane out and give me three good smashings across my hand. I used to say to myself, 'I wish I could get there early and miss that cane'. I used to tell my mother 'bout it, an' she used to say, 'He'll get tired, he'll get tired, son'. But 'twas me taking the punishment. And he used to glory in it, an' my fingers used to swell up, an' they'd be like sausages all swollen up.

A number of Labour-controlled local authorities banned corporal punishment in their schools. This was largely due to pressure from school students and the Society To Oppose Physical Punishment (STOPP).

Nevertheless in 1984 a survey of 2,119 secondary schools (45% of the total in England and Wales) revealed that 80% of secondary schools still beat children. Only in 1987 was corporal punishment finally made illegal in maintained schools.

In fifteenth century Italy a ten-year-old boy called **Morelli** resisted this barbaric tradition in his own way:

> He went to school of his own accord to learn to read and write. When he had received many blows from his teacher he left and wouldn't go back. And so by himself, without any intermediary, he changed teachers many times and with some he would make a bargain and get promises not to be beaten. If the bargain was kept he stayed, if not, he departed.

Regimentation at school: South Africa

I don't know why people say these are the best days of your life, because you're always under someone else's command — at school or at home. — **Fourteen-year-old girl**

Boys don't do any of the work at home and they are allowed to get away with it. — **Fifteen-year-old girl**

Matchgirl's Strike against the poverty wages of young working women, 1888

Children are inevitably involved in political issues, whether they be the more general ones of society as a whole, like unemployment or racism, or more specific ones such as school uniform or corporal punishment. Consequently they also engage in political action, whether it be collective industrial action like the 1888 Matchgirls' Strike over victimisation, dangerous conditions and poor pay (one sixteen year old reported taking home 4 shillings a week, of which 2 shillings paid her rent while she survived on a steady diet of bread, butter and tea), or the individual strike action of a boy in northern Ghana:

> Yindol, aged about 11, an intelligent and enterprising lad, was already giving his father valuable asistance, both in the care of livestock and in farming. When the great dances came round, Yindol wanted a new loincloth. His father refused to buy him one, whereupon Yindol went on strike, neglected the chickens, the donkeys, the goats, and even refused to go to the bush farm even after a beating. In the end his father had to yield. 'Bii la mar buurt' (the boy has justice on his side), he said, when he told the story.

Map legend:
- Saladin's Mohammedan Empire.
- Eastern Empire.
- Christian Kingdoms of Antioch & Tripoli.

The Children's Crusade is a remarkable example of children's organisation. It was a peaceful movement of the poor, mainly farm workers and shepherds, organised by themselves and clearly presenting a challenge to both church and state.

The German crusade began in the spring of 1212 near Cologne and was led by a twelve-year-old boy called **Nicholas** who wore a tau-cross as a sign of miraculous power. He led about 20,000 boys and girls, and older people, over 700 miles across the Alps to Italy, travelling over 20 miles a day. Many died on the way or turned back, but about 7,000 reached Genoa and some continued to Brindisi at the foot of Italy. They believed that God would transport them with dry feet to the Holy Land. The crusade may well have influenced **St Francis** in his attempt later in the same year to gain peaceful access to Jerusalem.

A similar movement in France was led by another twelve year old boy called **Stephen**, who entered Paris at the head of a crowd of 30,000. The king ordered them to return home and the Bishop of Paris also saw the threat to the established order when children and peasants take such actions. He said to one of them:

> My child, you claim to serve God's natural order better than we do, but you are mistaken. For in this order parents command children, priests bless, knights fight, peasants labour and children obey. If we let children preach and command, do you not see that the order is reversed? The devil has led you into a trap and you have fallen into it.

Richard II, the first known portrait

His advice fell on deaf ears as children were active in all the peasant uprisings in the Middle Ages. Unfortunately they could also be on the side of oppression. In 1381 **King Richard II** was only 15 when he betrayed the Peasants' Revolt and had their leaders, **Wat Tyler** and **John Ball**, killed along with 7,000 others.

Another example of a twelve year old exercising political power comes from the fifteenth century:

> King Edward scraped together every penny he could lay hands on, and he dispatched commissions of array for twenty-two counties, the whole southern half of England. Customarily a half-dozen or more men were appointed commissioners for each county. In this case, however, Richard, Duke of Gloucester, was made sole commissioner for nine of the twenty-two counties. It appears that Richard, in his twelfth year, had been entrusted by his royal brother with the surprising responsible charge of levying troops from a quarter of the realm.

Henry V served as a general in his father's army, conducting the war against Wales, when he was only fourteen. In the seventeenth and eighteenth centuries children travelled round Europe and America as Quaker preachers. Among their number were **William Hunt**, aged 14, **George Newlan**, aged 12, **Ellis Lewis**, aged 13, and **Christina Barclay**, aged 14. There were Methodist boy preachers in the eighteenth and nineteenth centuries. In the American War of Independence there were fourteen year old midshipmen and there was a sixteen year old who commanded his own ship.

Doll in sailor suit: children also served in the armed forces

More recently many children were involved in supporting the 1984/5 Miners' Strike. As **Cathrine Church**, treasurer of Bentley Womens' Action Group in Yorkshire, said, "You will find children of all ages who actively supported the strike".

Right at the beginning of the strike there was a report on the radio that 150 Scottish pupils had walked out of school to join the miners' picket, only to be turned back by the police.

At the beginning of November 1984 Barnsley miners came down to London to collect in Clapham. They were surprised at the generosity of Londoners and even more amazed when a group of kids tipped their Guy Fawkes collection into the miners' bucket.

Miners' children invented songs such as "We are the miners' kids" and, in good time for Christmas, "While miners watched their pits by night".

In September a letter arrived from my nephew, who was twelve years old at the time, and lives in Stepney:

> Dear Martin
>
> Thank you for sending me the miners' stickers. Now my school is well and truly behind the miners. But now I am short of stickers and other true blue schools have to be hit. So please can you put some more stickers in the envelope enclosed.
>
> Yours faithfully
> **Oliver**

Drawing by Leanne Platek, aged 11, Staffordshire

A miner from Askern in Yorkshire told me his thirteen year old daughter, **Joanne,** was actively supporting the strike. She later wrote me a long letter, under different headings. This is what she wrote about picketing:

> My dad goes picketing every day. He usually goes to pits in Nottingham, in his friend's car (Alan). He goes with Alan and Billy. He shouldn't go picketing now because he has been arrested, but he does. He is to go to court on the 19th December 1984. I go to school each day wondering what is happening to my dad. 'Will he be home tonight when I go home?'
>
> Quite a few times my dad has come home with bruises on his arms and legs (more bruises than what I get at hockey).

This strike means a lot to me and my dad because he and all other men who are on strike are fighting against job losses and for their children's future. Although I am eleven I understand most of the strike. I like going on the picket line with my mum and dad and friends, and the boys in blue watching us. Also going on marches holding placards with COAL NOT DOLE and SAVE JOBS. **Leanne**, age 11, Staffordshire

There were times when it was hard at school. They made fun of me and said I would not get much for Christmas. But I would go through it all again. **Jason**, age 11, Wales

When constabulary duty's to be done,
A policeman's lot is not a happy one
W.S. GILBERT

In Kent I met a fifteen-year-old girl called **Ellie Bence**. Her father was a miner at Snowdon Colliery and her mother had spent much of the strike speaking at meetings. Her grandfather was in the General Strike of 1926 and had cycled down to Kent from Scotland in 1931 to find work. Her friend **Lisa**, also fifteen, said she was on the picket line when both her brother and her father were arrested. They all live in the pit village of Aylesham.

Ellie had been writing poems about the strike and she told me she was going to read them out in the miners' club during a performance by the Ragged Trousered Cabaret. The cabaret commanded much attention but when Ellie got up to the mike there was complete silence. She dedicated one of the poems to her father and read it with great power and confidence:

A job so dirty and dangerous
Conditions worse than hell
A stench of cold and darkness
Is all a nose can smell
All an ear hears is the Whistling and Banging of work
All the men can feel is tiredness and dirt
All the eye can see is a black and lonely cave
Their legs and arms so heavy
Their backs and shoulders grazed
And when I ask my Father Why he is Striking once again
He answers Oh So Calmly for the Unity of Men.

Ellie Bence reads her poems

The final poem she sang to the tune of *Amazing Grace*. People stood to applaud. Her father was in tears. Ellie was overwhelmed.

> It's taken time to build our lives
> Our strong community
> But strength and love will see us through
> To keep our unity
> For many months we've fought like dogs
> And now the pit's a part
> Of our lives and history
> The centre of my heart
>
> As time goes on and things get hard
> I know we will pull through
> And years from now our sons will mine
> It's all the thanks to you.

Earlier she had been interviewed for the radio and had this to say:

> "I just see myself as a miner's daughter. That's political enough for me. It's been terrible at school because most of the teachers - I'd say 80% - are Conservative. There's only a few that understand how the children feel. A lot of them think that we don't understand what's going on, politically and everything. Then there's been quite a few teachers belittling miners' children in front of the class. Recently there was a third year girl who had a 'Kent women against pit closures' tee-shirt on and this very conservative teacher made her take it off. Then he got her up in the front of the class and he said, 'How much money is your father getting? What do you think about the strike?' And for a thirteen year old it's ever such a frightening experience, especially coming from someone so much older than you. But they don't ask me or my friends cos we're a lot older and we really understand and we know how to answer."

Drawing by Susan Sandhu, aged 8, Nottinghamshire

Chapter Seven

SCHOOL'S OUT

Children have as much need for a revolution as the proletariat have. **William Morris**

The idea of the general strike caught the mood of the people. It struck their sense of humour. The idea was infectious. The children struck in the schools, and such teachers as came, went home again from deserted class-rooms. The general strike took the form of a great national picnic. And the idea of the solidarity of labour, so evidenced, appealed to the imagination of all. **Jack London**, *The Iron Heel* , 1907

With the development of schooling much of children's political action began to centre on the school, though not all has been as violent as the murder of a teacher by his pupils around the year 400 AD. Apparently the boys killed him by stabbing and piercing his body with the little 'styles' which they used to write on their wax tablets.

The early twentieth century saw two remarkable examples of children's political action in British schools. The first was the wave of children's strikes that took place in 1911 which were amazing for their scale, as they were reported all over the country. They reflect the children's solidarity and also the influence of the press (though clearly not in the way intended by most of the journalists concerned!). The second was the Burston school strike of 1914 which is important for the length of time it lasted, for the way in which the whole Labour Movement became involved, and for the fact that it was organised by thirteen-year-old **Violet Potter**.

In 1911 children's strikes took place in over 60 major towns and cities in Britain. Clearly they were closely connected with other working class political action, as the *Birmingham Daily Mail* reported on the 14th September:

Violet Potter, aged 13, when she was the children's strike leader

Formerly boys drew their inspiration from tales of adventure or the more romantic episodes related in their history books. The advent of the picture press and the cinematograph has brought them into closer contact with current events. Their conduct of the strike reveals a close intimacy with the methods employed in the railway and dockers' strikes.

Similarly the *Hull Daily News* on 13th September:

> Hull escapes little in the way of trouble, and so it came to
> pass yesterday that hundreds of school-boys came out on
> strike. Hull has thus been involved in practically every phase
> of unrest which has troubled the country during the past few
> months. For weeks there has been a feeling of anxiety as to
> what might happen next. First, the sailors and dockers; then
> the millers, cement workers, timber workers, railway men,
> news-boys, factory girls and now the school-boys.

The pupils held meetings, organised flying pickets, marched and
demonstrated, organised strike committees and issued statements
to the press.

In Montrose they drew up a list which included:

> Steam heating apparatus;
> Age limit fixed at fourteen;
> Shorter hours;
> Potato-lifting holidays;
> No home lessons;
> Abolition of the strap;
> Free pencils and rubbers.

At Darlington they demanded "one hour schooling in the morning
and one in the afternoon, and one shilling per week for
attendance".

Hull strikers demanded "an extra half day holiday weekly,
monitors to be paid a penny a week, and all to leave school at the
age of 13".

At Leicester they carried banners bearing the words "We want
30s a week and less hours per day".

At Newcastle "a number of boys met and in addition to asking
for the abolition of the cane and establishment of a weekly
half-holiday, requested that a penny should be given, out of the
rates, to each boy every Friday".

The retaliation after the strikes were over was often vicious. In
Cardiff's dockland area the West Indian leader of the school
strikes, **Clyde Roberts**, said:

> When we got back, we had a schoolmaster, name was
> Mr Hobbs, so I got singled out. And he said 'I'm going to

put the fear of God into you!' He did. There was a boy on
each of the arms, legs, over the desk, and he didn't half
whack me. He was the only schoolmaster that I can say I was
frightened of. I was dead scared of him after that lot.

An earlier nationwide wave of strikes took place in 1889,
starting in Scotland and spreading right down to London, Bristol
and Cardiff. In south London the schoolboys who took part
decided not to return to school unless their four demands were
met:

Free education, one free meal a day, no home lessons and
no caning. The boys further resolved that they - and girls-
should meet at a later date in the same place, parade
through the streets and extend the proposed strike to the
whole of London.

A STRIKER ARRESTED BY HIS MOTHER.

At the same time in the east end, according to the *Pall Mall Gazette,* "four or five hundred boys who marched through the streets in the neighbourhood of Bethnal Green making the street echo with their cries of 'No more cane' were headed by a couple of boys carrying red flags and wearing scarlet liberty caps".

Many other children's strikes occurred in the early part of this century, to stop teachers being sacked, to retain local schools, to provide free transport - often with the active support of parents.

In 1914 pupils in Herefordshire supported the National Union of Teachers in their demand for a pay rise. In response to the union's strategy of mass resignations the local education authority brought in new teachers, many of them unqualified. Pupils refused to be taught by these teachers and 70 schools were forced to close. The most violent scenes occurred at Ledbury Girls' School, where a riot developed in which desks were overturned and the new headmistress was chased off the premises by a crowd of girls chanting "Blackleg". The action was eventually successful, the teachers reinstated and awarded a substantial salary increase.

Also in 1914, the most famous children's strike took place at Burston in Norfolk. The two teachers in the village school, **Mrs** and **Mr Higdon**, were Christian Socialists, and Tom Higdon was particularly active as county secretary of the Agricultural Workers Union. In 1914 they were dismissed by the managers (made up of the vicar and local landowners) on trumped-up charges of assaulting children.

The children, led by a 13-year-old girl called **Violet Potter**, came out on strike in support of their teachers, and the other villagers supported them too.

The children organised marches and demonstrations round the village, playing mouth organs and tin whistles, banging pots and pans, and singing:

> We'll all go the same way home
> All the whole collection
> In the same direction
> We'll all cling together like the ivy
> On the old garden wall.

Painting of the Burston Strike School

One small boy wrote: "God sent fine weather a' purpose for us strikers." *It was to be the longest strike in history.*

The issue was taken up by the whole British Labour Movement, culminating in May 1917 with the opening of the Burston Strike School, funded by trade unionists, which continued to operate up until the Second World War. Violet Potter remembered the speech she made at the opening:

> I stood on the steps of this school in front of crowds of
> people at seventeen years of age, and opened this school. I
> remember what I said to this day. 'With joy and thankfulness
> I declare this school open to be for ever a school of
> freedom.'

The building still exists and has been renovated. One of the girls who took part in the strike describes what happened:

> We came on strike on April 1st, 1914. We came on strike
> because our Governess and Master were dismissed from the
> Council School unjustly. The parson got two Barnardo
> children to say that our Governess had caned them and

slapped their faces, but we all know she did not. Then our Governess lit a fire one wet morning to dry some of our clothes without asking the Parson. So the head ones said that our Governess and Master had better be got rid of. They had their pay sent and two days' notice to leave the school. Governess did not know we were going on strike. She bought us all some Easter eggs and oranges the last day we were at the Council School.

Violet Potter brought a paper to school with all our names on it, and all who were going on strike had to put a cross against their name. Out of seventy-two children sixty-six came out on strike.

The first morning our mothers sent the infants because they thought they did not matter, but in the afternoon they too stopped away and only six answered the bell.

The next morning the sixty-six children lined up on the Crossways. We all had cards round our necks and paper trimmings. We marched past the Council School and round 'The Candlestick'. When we got to the foster-mother's house she came out with a dustpan and brush to 'tin' us, but when she saw our mothers she ran in. She put a card in her window with 'Victory' on it, but she has not got it yet. Some of our parents gave us cake and drink and many other things. When we got to the Crown Common we had a rest. Mrs Boulton, the lady at the Post Office, gave us some lemonade and sweets and nuts. She also gave us a large banner and several flags. At twelve o'clock we went home for dinner. At one we marched again. When we got to one of the foster-mother's friends (who is a foster-mother too) she jumped up from behind a hedge and began to 'tin' us. When we hooted her she said she would summons us, but it has not happened yet.

Foundation stone of the new school at Burston, funded by the Labour Movement

Mr Starr, the Attendance Officer, sent our mothers a paper saying if they did not send their children to school they would be summoned but our mothers did not care about the papers; some put them on sticks and waved them. We had our photos taken several times. We marched each day. Two of our mothers asked Governess to come and take prayers on the Common with the children, then she came each morning. Half a dozen policemen stood about the road, but there was no need for them.

One day a policeman went round to twenty houses with summonses because we had not been to school. The day we were to appear at Court all the big children dressed up and went to the Crossways. We started for Court about half past nine. As we were going along we sang our old Strike Song. Before we started we had oranges and chocolate.

When we got down to Diss several people were lined up each side of the street. We left our parents at the Court and we went into the Park. Mrs Robert Wilby brought us some refreshments, ginger beer, etc. Some of the girls went to the Court to see what the time was. There a man took their photos. The fine was half a crown each. When our mothers came out of Court we went into the Market Place and had some bread and cheese to eat on the way home. Mrs Boulton gave us some chocolate. Then we started home. When we got half-way home we sat down and had a rest and ate our cakes. We got home about six o'clock.

The next day our mothers thought we might begin school on the Common while it was fine weather. We had school on the Common a little while, then we went into the very cottage that the Barnardo children had lived in for a year and a half.

Our mothers lent stools, tables, chairs, etc. Mr Ambrose Sandy came and white-washed it out and mended the windows. He put a ladder up so that we could go upstairs. Our mothers were soon summoned again. This time the children did not go. They went a little way, then they came back. This time the fine was five shillings each. There were thirty-two of our parents summoned. Our parents did not have to pay a penny of the fine, it was all collected on the Green and in the streets. At night we went to Diss to meet our parents. When we got there we had some ginger beer. A man took our photos for the living pictures. Then we went to see them; they were very good. Mr Sullings gave us a free performance. **Emily Wilby** (age 13)

Tom Higdon: photograph taken by his brother

Tom Higdon also gave his version of what happened on that April day 1914. He describes the children's courage and determination, their good humour and solidarity:

> The bell rang still more loudly and wildly as the juvenile procession approached nearer and nearer. School gates and doors were thrown wide open to give free and unimpeded admission, while police and School Managers posted themselves on both sides and in the middle of the road below with a view to intimidating the processionists and preventing their progress past the School. But the youngsters, doubtless feeling that there was strength in their numbers, showed not the least sign of fear as they approached this imposing posse of police and Education

magnates, but marched confidently forward to the tune of - and singing -

> 'Come, cheer up, my lads, 'tis to glory we steer,
> The prize more than all to an Englishman dear;
> 'Tis to honour we call you, not press you like slaves -
> For who are so free as the sons of the waves?'

Police and Education magnates fell back perforce to let the daring rebels pass, never venturing, of course, to lay a hand on them, and again wave after wave of cheers arose from the triumphant rebel band."

Young strikers at the First Anniversary celebrations, 1st April 1915

The renewed interest in children's rights and the political side of childhood has largely been a result of the political actions of school children since the early 1970s. These include overt political activities such as demonstrations, leafleting and strikes, and more indirect forms such as large-scale truancy and disruption of lessons.

By 1972 in Britain two national organisations of school students had been developed: the more overtly political Schools Action Union which was eventually controlled by Maoists, and the more trade union type organisation of the NUSS under the wing of the National Union of Students.

The SAU was particularly active in organising strikes in London. They began with a handful of schools in Paddington and on May 17th several thousand school children went on strike and marched through London. The *Guardian* put the numbers at 2,000 and *The Times* at 2,500. Both papers were scathing and referred to the children playing truant. The children raised the following demands:

*No victimisation - reinstate all suspended and expelled students.
*No more detentions, canings and compulsory school uniforms.
*Free school milk, free and decent school dinners.
*Rules to be decided and enforced by the whole school.
*Maintenance grants of £10 a week for all those staying on at school after their 15th birthday.
*Working class studies to be introduced, including day release to get different work experience.
*A job for all on leaving school.

The previous week 1,000 children in Camden schools had walked out carrying banners and shouting 'No school uniform' and 'No caning'. They joined 4,000 other school students at a rally organised by the SAU.

The SAU did not last long, and the NUSS folded at the end of the decade. Nevertheless political action took place in countless schools, only some of it organised by the NUSS and only some of it reported in the press.

School students went on strike at Wanstead High against cuts in education and oversized classes. They walked out of St Bonaventure's in Forest Gate because the heating system had broken down. Two school students were arrested while distributing leaflets outside the City of Leeds High School. Girls in a Nottingham school walked out after the headmaster complained that they looked like 'tarts'. Students at schools such as Clissold Park in Stoke Newington and Trinity Comprehensive in Canning Town handed out pamphlets attacking the fascist policies of the National Front.

Outside an Ipswich school in 1978 National Front supporters beat a hasty retreat when set upon by a crowd of angry pupils. Two Front supporters tried to give out leaflets but they were spat on and their literature torn from their hands.

When the school leaving age went up to sixteen, a group of fifth-year girls from Kidbrooke in south London walked out of school, taking with them as many others as they could, protesting about being forced to stay at school when they wanted to leave. Once out of school, they marched to several other schools in the area, wanting to bring out all the schools on strike and planning to march to Westminster to put their case to Parliament.

In 1974 black students from Tulse Hill school in south London organised and demonstrated against police harassment and wrongful arrest:

> They formed a committee, the Black Students' Action Collective (Black Sac), and invited participation from four other schools in the area in which they knew they had support and friends. They called a one day strike of pupils from schools. They had very little machinery of organisation.

Immigration in Britain would lead to 'rivers of blood': Enoch Powell

They knew only that the case and trial of Robin Sterling had excited a lot of comment in the school, and felt that teachers at Tulse Hill, and at other schools were, for the first time, clearly on the side of the victimised and not on the side of the police.

On the day of the strike a hundred black youth from my school, joined by sixty white friends, declared their intention to come out on strike. A few teachers went along with them. In fact the headmaster, having learnt of the strike through the leaflets that were circulating in our school, was in favour of teachers going with them to ensure that they got into as little trouble as possible. The headmaster of Tulse Hill had taken no such stance. He locked the gates of the school. The leaders of the strike demonstration were from his school and they led the 800 strong demonstration past the gates of several schools in Southwark and Brixton. They were joined by a few hundred more. The demonstration reached Tulse Hill. It was break time and the youth swarmed out into the playground and over the walls to join the demo. **Farrukh Dhondy**

In 1983 school students closed down their school in Bradford in protest against racism. In the centre of the same city in February 1985 school children held a demonstration after being told their lunches were to be cancelled because of the teachers' industrial action. Traffic was halted as they marched to the town hall. A boy of thirteen had a thumb amputated after it was trapped in a wrought-iron gate as security men closed it to stop the children storming the hall. Police were called to round up the two hundred, aged twelve to sixteen, and escort them back to Carlton Bolling School, about a mile away. More than a thousand pupils refused to return to their desks after the lunch break and some of those joining the march carried banners which they had made the previous night. One fifteen year old boy said: "We are getting the worst of the teachers' dispute. It is not right. We say: No dinners - No lessons."

School students have produced many leaflets to aid their campaigns. One produced by the NUSS had the title 'Keep the Young National Front out of our Schools. 1930s: HITLER YOUTH 1977: YNF'. Another entitled 'School Students Charter' had the following demands:

1. NO CORPORAL PUNISHMENT
2. NO SCHOOL UNIFORM
3. NO PETTY RULES
4. NO PREFECTS
5. NO SECRET FILES

The NUSS also produced a magazine called *Blot*, and more recently a collective of young women still at school brought out *Shocking Pink*. In the second issue of the magazine they produced a manifesto:

At the moment the magazines are mainly run by older women (and men), many of whom are completely out of touch with what young women want. They keep saying that they are giving us what we want. But *we* don't want it. In any case, they can't know what young women want, because there's no alternative at the moment for them to choose from.

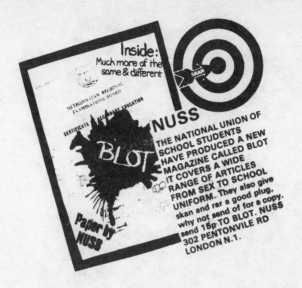

There are many issues which particularly concern younger women. It is not *us* who are ageist. We are forced into certain situations because of age. We have fewer rights than older women. Our social and everyday lives are controlled by laws and attitudes which presume we have to be 'protected', but in fact stop us from doing what we want to do: age of consent, entertainment and licensing laws, employment regulations etc. We need a magazine in which young women write about these extra restrictions.

The magazine will be run by women working together, mainly young women. Young women have little or no opportunity to show what they are capable of.

We want to show that we can do it on our own. We want an alternative magazine because *Jackie* and *Oh Boy* etc don't give a realistic impression of our lives. None of them encourage us to feel complete or independent as young women. They encourage us to feel that you have to lean on somebody (usually a boy) or something (usually clothes and make-up).

They don't give us credit for intelligence, like the rest of the media, they presume that we are only interested in clothes, cooking, the home and family, and getting our man. We're interested in some of these things but not in the way they constantly present them.

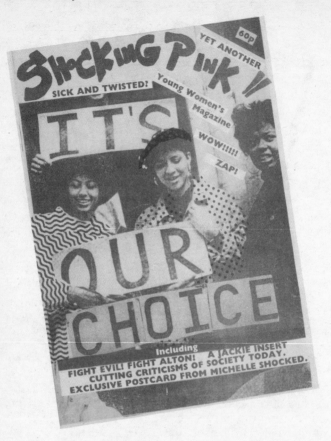

On 25th April 1985 the Youth Trade Union Rights Campaign called a national school student strike in protest against the government's Youth Training Scheme. It had been organised at the Young Socialists' Conference a few weeks earlier in Blackpool where 200 YS members formed the School Students Action Committee and then linked up with the YTURC. The aim was to found School Student Unions at each school and eventually revive a national union. They claimed there were 200,000 strikers in 60 towns and cities.

Sixty Merseyside pupils who met regularly during the two weeks prior to the strike helped distribute 20,000 leaflets urging school children to join the strike.

In Liverpool four thousand pupils marched to the city's Pier Head to be addressed by Labour MP **Terry Fields**. In Manchester and Cardiff a thousand pupils marched in each city. In Reading forty-one boys were arrested while trying to spread the strike to Southland Girls' School. In Caerphilly three hundred children marched through the town and police reported "severe disorder".

In London several local demonstrations took place. A hundred girls marched through the centre of Stratford in the East End. Five hundred children rallied in Lincoln's Inn Fields and marched to the Manpower Services Commission in nearby Holborn, accompanied by Labour MPs **Ernie Roberts** and **Harry Cohen**, and GLC deputy leader **John McDonnell**. Six children were arrested in Woolwich after hundreds had marched through the shopping centre despite a ban on their march.

In Stoke on Trent three children were arrested. In Barnsley five hundred children joined the protest. In Coventry two hundred. The national press was almost uniformly hostile to all these protests:

"Let's play strikes." **Daily Mail**

"Pupils' big strike action fizzles out into farce." **Daily Express**

"41 KIDS HELD AS POLICE QUELL SCHOOL RIOT."
The Sun

"School strike kids go on the rampage." **Daily Star**

"Pupils in school 'strike' arrested." **The Times**

The leader of the Labour Party called those involved "dafties". Later in the year at the Labour Party Conference a motion calling on Labour to recognise the school strike and to support the School Students' Union was defeated by 4,138,000 to 2,362,000 votes.

Chapter Eight

RACISM

If I'm with a white boy, say just on the way home from college, they shout in the street, 'What's it like to fuck a Paki?' or if I'm on my own or with other girls it's 'Here comes the Paki whore, come and fuck us Paki whores, we've heard you're really horny.' Or maybe they'll put it the other way round, saying that I'm dirty, that no one could possibly want to go to bed with a Paki. I can't tell you how degrading that gets to be, even when you've learnt to steel yourself to stand up to them and not cross the road when you see a group of white guys coming towards you. I don't think any white person can possibly identify with what it's like...... All the time they were shouting, 'Get the Paki whore, we're going to have a gang bang.' I have never been so scared. I was convinced I was going to be raped. **Sunjita**

In October 1977 the National Front announced the formation of a youth section, the Young National Front, to recruit school students into their membership and they published *Bulldog*, the organ of the East London Young National Front, a magazine which said 'distribute Bulldog in your school and annoy the Red teachers. You can upset the teachers and help the National Front at the same time. All youths should take part in Operation NF - spread the racialist word, distribute Bulldog or any NF literature in schools.' NUSS immediately produced our own leaflet to counter the NF campaign. It was headed 'Keep the YNF out of our schools' and we distributed 20,000 of them last term, mainly in schools in London where Bulldog had been circulated. **National Union of School Students**

Children have often been in the forefront of racist attacks and they have also resisted them. Despite the prevalence of many forms of racism, against Irish and Jewish people, for example, the main racist attacks today are against black people, Afro-Caribbeans and Asians.

*Olaudah Equiano, the first political leader of
Britain's black community (1745-1797): Kidnapped
in Nigeria and transported to the West Indies, bought
his freedom and campaigned throughout England
against the slave trade.*

There were Africans in Britain before the English came here.
Some were soldiers in the Roman army, others were slaves.
Among the troops defending Hadrian's wall in the third century
AD was a division of Moors, originally from North Africa and
stationed near Carlisle.

The remains of a young African girl were recently found in a
burial, dated about 1000 AD, in Norfolk. In the sixteenth and
seventeenth centuries black children were brought here from

'They keep saying that they are giving us what we want. But we don't want it'

Africa and the West Indies as servants, and there are continual references to them running away.

By the 1780s there were always at least fifty African school children, girls as well as boys, in Liverpool and the villages around. Most of them came from Liberia, the Ivory Coast and Ghana. They were sent by their parents to receive the advantage of a European elementary education. They were taught reading, writing, arithmetic and religion. The girls were also instructed in 'domestic duties' and needlework. African children were also educated in Bristol in the same period. There were 20,000 black people in London in 1764, and according to a writer in the *Gentleman's Magazine*:

> They cease to consider themselves as slaves in this free country, nor will they put up with an inequality of treatment.

Today black school students are a strong force in schools. Many have rejected the white European dominated curriculum and put on pressure for change. One of the first schools to respond was Tulse Hill Comprehensive in South London which organised a world history course around comparative studies of different kinds of contact between cultures. The materials used were classified by region and century, and by themes indicating different kinds of contact: cooperation (including Captain Cook and the Maoris, the Hindus and Mongols), exploitation (the Spanish and Incas), rejection, settlement, mission, forced movement (including transportation of white convicts as well as black slaves), voluntary movement, refuge (the Pilgrim Fathers and Huguenots), and resistance. In the fourth and fifth years the course dealt with Nazi Germany and the Second World War, with a special option on Commonwealth troops. Other topics included the Chinese Revolution, a history of British working people, and the history of the black experience.

Recently a number of local education authorities have issued guidelines on multicultural education and policy statements on anti-racist teaching. The Inner London Education Authority's Anti-Racist Guidelines aim to deal with:

*Physical assault against a person or group because of colour or ethnicity.
*Derogatory name-calling, insults and racist jokes.
*Racist graffiti or any other written insult.
*Provocative behaviour such as wearing racist badges or insignia.
*Bringing racist material such as leaflets, comics or magazines into the school or college.
*Making threats against a person or group because of colour or ethnicity.
*Racist comment in the course of discussion in lessons.
*Attempts to recruit other pupils and students to racist organisations and groups.

Black students make a forceful attack on institutional racism in our society, and particularly in our schools:

> It always amused other members of the class when our geriatric P.E. teacher called me 'Sambo' or made me climb the ropes 'because I was used to it'. Don't let anyone tell you that there aren't racists in the teaching profession, because I have come across a few.
>
> Whilst in my fourth year at the school, a prefect of the lower sixth form decided to start pulling his weight, but especially with me. He placed me in detention for various offences such as talking in cloisters, running etc. But one day the said prefect shouted 'Wog, come here' repeatedly in front of his friends. After his repeating the abuse for more times than I care to remember, I told him to 'fuck off'. The consequences of this reply were that he put me on his personal detention list and on the school detention list. I did not turn up to either detention, so he reported me to my form master. My form master asked me why I did not turn up and I told him the reason. His reply was that I should turn up to both detentions, otherwise I would be in serious trouble. As far as they were concerned, I was being justly treated for my actions. **David Lawson**

> My secondary school was very rigidly streamed, not only along class but also racial lines. In the top streams of every year up to the fifth year the pupils were predominantly white and middle class, in a school were the overwhelming majority of the children came from working-class homes and 50% were black (Afro-Caribbean/Asian). In my year, for instance, the two top streams each had one token black. At the other end of the scale, in the bottom streams 99% of the pupils were black with one or two token whites. This division was so blatant that even had we not been prompted we could hardly fail to notice the difference. The two streams were even geographically divided within the school. The school had two major wings. In one wing there were mainly large airy classrooms, in the other were smaller rooms and practical facilities such as Art, Needlework, Housework and Woodwork rooms. The lower streams were confined to this wing as these were the activities they spent most of their time on, while the A stream were being groomed for 'O' levels in the Arts.
>
> Many black girls left school with not even a CSE, but had a handful of certificates and medals for sporting triumphs. One of the ways in which we rebelled was to go to all the training lessons

and develop until it was known we were really good at some
event, and then on sports day when asked to compete we would
refuse. But although we were aware of the racism surrounding us
and challenged it whenever we could, as pupils we had little power
to effect any positive change. **Vincia Bennett**

It was on the day I saw snow for the first time in my life, and what was worse it was the first time I had to walk on it to get home, that I found a group of boys from a neighbouring school along with some of the girls from my school following me. I was trying very hard to walk along elegantly but without much success when I realised that they were shouting abuse which was directed at me. They were informing me that Pakis do not know how to walk and that they should go back home. Every time I slipped I would hear a loud roar of laughter from behind me. I tried to hurry but this only made matters worse. I slipped and fell which added more amusement to my audience's pleasure, by which time one of them shouted, 'Let's get the Paki', and they all started firing snowballs at me. I felt nothing but hatred for those people from that day onwards. That is a scene I remember every time it snows and it is a memory which will always remain with me. **Rani**

In 1986 a powerful response to racism was organised by Asian pupils at Daneford Boys School in East London. After a series of racist attacks had occurred in the school, the students formed self-defence groups and also developed their own political programme:

We made a list of demands of things that were important to Bengali boys. We wrote our own leaflets. We decided to form groups in the school to defend ourselves and fight the racists back. We had to demonstrate at the County Hall to fight the racists and get Bengali lessons for all boys. After all our struggling things started to get better. The racists were frightened by our power. All boys can now study their mother tongue. Bengali boys can have a better future in our school. Boys and girls from other schools will be joining our group. We want the police out of school. Teachers can have their policy. It will not be powerful until they stand by the students! **Abdul Hoque**, Bangladeshi United Youth Group, Daneford School

Chapter Nine

SEXISM AND HETEROSEXISM

The whole education of women ought to be relative to men. To please them, to be useful to them, to make themselves loved and honoured by them, to educate them when young, to care for them when grown, to counsel them, to console them and to make life sweet and agreeable to them — these are the duties of women at all times and what should be taught them from their infancy. **Jean Jacques Rousseau** 18th century

A son had been born! I felt neglected and when I ran to my father and threw my arms around his pillar-like legs, he shook me off and told me to go away. There seemed something wrong with me, something too deep to even cry about. **Agnes Smedley** 1929

Quite frankly I don't think mothers have the same right to work as fathers. If the good Lord had intended us to have equal rights to go out and work, he wouldn't have created man and woman. These are biological facts. Young children do depend on their mothers. **Patrick Jenkins**, Secretary of State for Social Services, 1979

Since the rebirth of the Women's Movement in the 1960s and 1970s ample evidence has been produced of the discrimination and prejudice against girls. Stereotyping begins at birth. Some hospitals even provide pink blankets for girls and blue ones for boys. Baby boys are encouraged to talk and act differently from girls. Nursery school reinforces the gender roles, partly through peer group pressure, as a nursery school teacher recounts:

In the nursery was a girl, Sheree, who wore trousers, shirts and had very short hair. She was aggressive and charged around the nursery, jumped on the rocking horse and rode it like fury. When she tired of this she watched the others and then came to me and said:
   'What else you got? Got any bikes?'

'The bikes are for outside a little later. How about playing with some puzzles or do a painting?'

'No.'

A boy, Darren, watched the boys push and fight their way to the garage. He walked to the home corner. Jane said:

'Want to be a baby, come and have dinner baby.'

He stood and cried.

Sheree and Darren could not relate to the two groups. Sheree, as time went on, related more and more to games with movement: racing, climbing, riding, and she tried to drag another girl with her. When this quiet little girl managed to give Sheree the slip, Sheree turned to a very popular, active boy and they developed a close friendship.

Darren drew more to the girls, dressing up in dresses and cooking the dinner. His mother came to see me, worried that he was too 'soft'. 'Even his little sister could bash him up'. She started to encourage other little boys from the nursery to go and play with Darren in their house. From then on Darren began to mix more with the boys and became more aggressive. He used to listen to the story alone and cried if it was sad, but now he sat and swung his legs, arm in arm with the core of lively boys. This little boy had been encouraged away from being sensitive, a girlish trait, to becoming a 'real' boy.

It was difficult to imagine Sheree integrated with the girls. As Christmas drew near her mum bought her some dresses and bobbles to wear in her hair. This had a dynamic effect:

'I'm as pretty as Kelly. Where's the mirror? Comb my hair, miss, and put my bobbles in.'

A girl who once had untidy hair, wore jeans and shirts, often had dirty hands, was becoming conscious of her own appearance which is a beginning to becoming 'feminine'.

Christopher, a boy in the nursery, used to cry desperately when he fell and cut himself. He hated to see blood. He is now, after a term of trips upside down from the climbing frame, becoming more controlled. However I found it was not due to the many falls he has had, but due to his mental approach. Twice I have heard him say to himself:

'Be a man, it don't really hurt. Only girls cry.'

Throughout schooling the emphasis on 'femininity', on girls only becoming wives and mothers, increases, and they are treated by the boys as inferior. The creation of the macho boy leads to the kind of masculinity which is normal in our society. It leads to battering, rape, treating girls and women as sex objects, male power in all our major institutions, feelings of competitiveness and natural superiority, and the general inability of boys to express feelings of tenderness and love.

In schools teachers give more attention to boys and usually reinforce the gender divisions in the curriculum. Boys dominate the space in schools - in classrooms, corridors and playgrounds. In classroom interaction boys ask and respond to twice as many questions as the girls. Boys harass girls verbally and physically. They sprawl into gangways "so you have to climb over them", lean over girls' desks, touch and pinch and prod, and poke pencils up through holes in laboratory stools while girls are sitting on them. They compel attention in class by groaning and sighing and making a show of restlessness whenever a girl is speaking.

In many places this is beginning to be challenged and some schools and local authorities have initiated anti-sexist policies. Stantonbury set up a group to combat sexism, but as one fifth form girl found in her survey of forty fifth-form students:

> Although Stantonbury does not encourage discrimination, 74% of girls and 64% of boys said they were treated differently. Girls are allowed to do the same subjects as boys, but they are treated quite differently in the classroom.

At home a similar gender discrimination usually occurs:

> Until we were old enough to choose our own clothes we were
> dressed as thought suitable for our gender. Nicki and I always
> wore skirts or dresses. Gregory never did. I remember him getting
> dressed for Sunday School when he was four and declaring that he
> was not going to wear 'that dress'. It was in fact a shirt with
> flowers on it. Dad used to complain that Nicki and I did not have
> shiny hair or smile. Nicki and I were sent to ballet classes and
> ballroom classes whereas Gregory went to judo classes. Gregory's
> masculinity was reinforced by being criticised for doing anything
> that could be considered feminine. Whenever he cried Dad would
> torment him by calling him 'Baby Boy', repeating these words
> over and over again.

*Boy with cricket bat and knickerbockers, girls in high-necked frocks, all in
elastic-sided boots*

I was aware from an early age that there was a supposed difference between men and women with regards to their mentality, that in the eyes of the world, especially men's eyes, men were superior. When I was five I hated being a girl because of the injustice connected with being so.

When I was nine I told the girls in my class at school whilst changing after a swimming lesson that I would never marry or have children. I was told that I would change my mind. I have not. **Anne Fullam**

Ursula LeGuin, in *The Left Hand of Darkness*, imagines a planet called Gethen where people are not identified as male or female: "When you meet a Gethenian you cannot and must not do what a bisexual naturally does, which is to cast him in the role of Man or Woman, while adopting towards him a corresponding role dependent on your expectations of the patterned or possible interactions between persons of the same or the opposite sex. Our entire pattern of socio-sexual interaction is non-existent here. They cannot play the game. They do not see one another as men or women. This is almost impossible for our imagination to accept.

What is the first question we ask about a newborn baby?"

'You're breaking the laws of nature!'

Meanwhile back on earth, a strong challenge to stereotyped gender roles and heterosexism comes from lesbian and gay young people:

> When I was little, I always thought I would get married, have children, and stay home cooking, cleaning and doing all the things housewives do. I expected such a future until I turned fifteen and started dating. I began to see that there were other things to do. I also began to notice homosexual couples and how happy they seemed. I really envied them and wondered why people didn't like them.
>
> I went to a Catholic high school where they actually said being a homosexual was a terrible sin. I had always been told that it was wrong and dirty, and that homosexuals were perverted and disgusting. I never believed it was wrong or dirty, but I never thought I might be, or have potential to be, gay. All I knew was that I envied them and wished I could be as sure of myself as they seemed to be of themselves.

Diane

I Came Out in Class!

In retrospect, I've always known I was a dyke, since I was about four — that's when I first remember 'falling in love' with a woman. I kept on falling in love with them from then on. I did get a crush on a boy when I was about ten — except he looked like a girl, and anyway, I was still into various women at the same time. At about twelve, I went to my mother and said, 'Do you think I'm a lesbian?' I was beginning to think it was a bit strange that I never fell in love with boys. My poor mother, who'd been thinking, 'I wonder if she's a lesbian?' said, 'Oh no, of course not, it's very normal at your age, most girls get these kinds of crushes.' **Bronwen**

Girls in the East End, 1930s

An example of heterosexism operating in school is given by a gay teacher from a London comprehensive, describing a thirteen year old girl who developed a love for a girl a year younger than herself who was at the same school:

> She would skip lessons in order to be near her. This is by no means an unusual occurrence among heterosexual children at school. It is usually dealt with by having the child put on report. There is no moralising, nor any questioning of whether the boy or girl really has sexual feelings towards the person of the opposite sex. After all, such behaviour is considered perfectly 'natural' and might even be tacitly encouraged as signs of 'young love'. What happened to this lesbian girl in a similar situation? She was put on report to the headmistress, but the year head of the younger girl took it upon herself to call in a policewoman, who explained to the two girls the sickness of lesbianism. The year head described the older girl as 'sick', and virtually forbade the younger girl from seeing her. I brought up the subject with the pastoral head of the school. 'Of course, you know the problem with Susan', she said confidently, 'she's a les.' The girl soon became notorious in the staffroom tittle-tattle. She acquired the status of a wanted criminal, being checked on from lesson to lesson. Rather than hear her natural tendencies described as sick, the girl truanted from school completely.

Teachers and local education authorities are at last beginning to look at how to tackle heterosexism in school. The Labour Party in the London borough of Haringey was elected to power on a manifesto committed to fight heterosexism in schools. It promised to finance classroom projects promoting positive images of lesbians and gays, and to back teachers and students who 'come out' at school.

An organisation, independent of the council, called *"Positive Images"*, is also campaigning for lesbian and gay rights in Haringey. They have produced a leaflet explaining what is meant by 'positive images' in schools:

> *Teachers preventing anti-lesbian and anti-gay terms of abuse and name-calling, in the same way as they should prevent racist remarks.

'Friends and relatives sometimes react strangely when you come out'

   *Supporting lesbian and gay teachers and students who choose to be open about their sexuality.
   *Including the subject in in-service training for all teachers and staff.
   *Discussing sexuality where it is relevant in other lessons, for example, in studying the work of lesbian and gay writers (Marlowe, Woolf, Forster, Auden etc.).
   *Looking at materials used in teaching and removing the ones which are heterosexist or homophobic.
   *Making available useful information on sexuality in school libraries, in the form of leaflets, books and 'pulp romances'.
   *Providing skilled counsellors who can discuss this issue with pupils.

Some curriculum materials are now available to counteract the pervading heterosexist stereotypes of lesbian and gay people. One example is *Jenny Lives With Eric and Martin*, translated from the Danish, and published by Gay Men's Press in 1983. It tells the story, in words and photographs, of a girl who lives with her father and his male lover.

Jenny, living with Eric and Martin

This book, in particular, and Haringey's policy, in general, have produced a predictable backlash. The Haringey Parents' Rights Group was set up, "incensed about this approach to teaching", and they organised demonstrations and boycotts of the schools. In October 1986 they held a public book-burning of copies of *Jenny Lives with Eric and Martin*. The local Conservative party, under the title of the 'Campaign for Normal Family Life', has also attacked the policy.

Eventually the whole issue was debated in Parliament, as reported by the *Guardian* in October 1986:

> **Mrs Sally Oppenheim** (Con. Gloucester) said too much emphasis was given in many schools to 'irrelevant and damaging sex education' and added: 'There should be fundamental facts of life,

birds and bees . . . sex education for children at around the age of
nine or ten . . . followed at the age of twelve or thirteen by a
further class which may refer to homosexuality, describing it as
abnormal or undesirable, but which must refer to the health
hazards which arise.' **Mr Clement Freud**, for the Liberals, said:
'I'm sorry that anybody on any side of the House should argue
against sex education for children because I believe that the child's
right to know should over-ride the parent's right to obscure.'

Chapter Ten

DISABILITY

Schools attended by children with disabilites should provide them with an education which enables the fullest development of their abilities. They should receive the best possible preparation for an integrated life in the community after they leave school. They should not suffer from over-protection and low expectations and should not be segregated in special schools unless it can be shown that these provide the best opportunity for their education and social development. The **Greater London Council**'s Charter for People with Disabilities

I n this century children with disabilities have usually been separated from other children and put in homes, institutions and special schools. 3% of children in England and Wales are in special schools.

The 1981 Education Act recommended that they be integrated into mainstream schools. But this recommendation has to be seen in the context of education cuts, when it is hardly likely that money will be spent on adapting schools, providing adequate facilities and retraining teachers. The extent of the changes which would have to be made becomes clear from only a brief extract from the pamphlet produced by the National Union of Teachers in 1977, entitled *Special Education in Ordinary Schools :*

> Close attention must of course be paid to safety. Switches, sockets and plugs must be situated in accessible, but not dangerous positions, safety glass should be used for all glass fittings, and floors should be smooth and non-slippery. Passages should be wide enough for two wheelchairs to pass, and ramps installed where necessary. Fire alarms should be fitted with visual as well as audible warnings (ie flashing lights), and rails should be installed at suitable heights throughout the school. Toilets should be adapted for special needs, which may mean widening the cubicles, supplying hand rails and providing mirrors on the floor of certain

water closets to help paraplegic children attend to their personal hygiene. Provision should also exist for large free areas for movement and general activity, away from teaching areas, and there should be adequate room for the storage of equipment, and for therapy to be carried out. In machine workshops the extraction of dust and fumes is vital for all children, but is most important for the asthmatic and other physically handicapped children. Similar safeguards should also be applied in science laboratories.

Multi-handicapped and physically handicapped children also need more space in the classroom, and the Union believes six square metres to be the minimum required per disabled child.

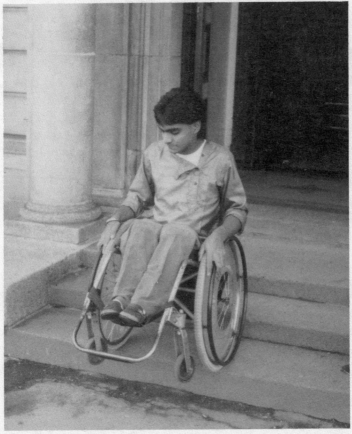

Jaspal Dhani negotiates steps

Getting in and out: cars and phone boxes pose problems for Jaspal Dhani
(above) *and Beena Bhugtiar* (opposite)

Pupils at a special school in Newham describe what it is like to have
disabilities:

> With my disability the problems arose even before I entered the
> school gates. Although many of my fellow pupils lived further
> from the school than I did, they were more able to accomplish the
> journey than I was. This problem is one which is relatively easy to
> overcome. Firstly with the assistance of my parents and later from
> the local council, transport was arranged to and from the school.
> My school, like many of the large comprehensives in the area, not
> only spread outwards but upwards as well — two tower blocks
> consisting of six flights of stairs leading to three of the four
> classrooms on each floor. To reach the fourth classroom you must
> ask permission to go through another teacher's class. This was not
> always advisable and one soon became aware of which teachers
> would say yes and which were not worth asking. The alternative
> to this was to go back down the stair-case on one side and back up
> on the other. My problems were thought to be solved when I was
> given a room on the ground floor where I stayed. The theory
> behind this plan was the work would be brought to me during
> each lesson. This, however, understandably proved to be too
> much bother for the teachers involved, having either to leave the

complete class or interrupt another pupil's study. **Wendy Hawkes**, aged 16

Many shops have a step of about 30cm with a door on top of it. To me this is one of the worst problems because you can't open the door and get up the step at the same time. This is far more difficult when the door has a spring on it. The problems of getting around in the streets mainly occur when the kerb is too high. Let's say a person is on the high street and the street is crowded. Now when the street is full of people it is not easy getting up a kerb of 15 inches without hitting someone who's passing by.

The GLC taxi card has opened a new road for many people. On this card you pay £1 for every £6 showing on the meter. Using this it could cost a person £1 for a five minute ride, so it would be cheaper if they could use the bus, but they can't because the new buses have two-way swinging doors which are about 20-30 inches off the ground. Not only this, you are faced with another large step in the door way, followed by a large pole, which not even Big Daddy could get round. Then the gangway is too narrow! **Jaspal Dhani**, aged 15

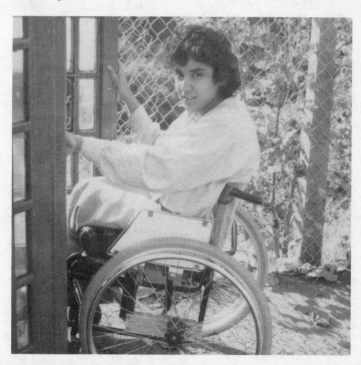

If someone sees a disabled person with family or friends they almost always walk up to the able-bodied person and say, 'What's wrong with her/him?' — nice and loud so that the whole street can hear them, as if they have a right to know. **Jane Carberry**, aged 16

If you're in a wheelchair you will always find some young kid coming up to you saying. 'I wish I was in your position, doing wheelies and taking my chair everywhere I go.' But believe me, they don't know how lucky they are. They're not the ones who when they were younger kept dwelling on the thought of when they would go out on their own, and not with the family, even to the shop round the corner. Then if they did go out they would always get someone who would break their confidence by calling them names. And then this kid was left there thinking, 'Do I really want to bother learning to do wheelies just to get insulted?' **Beena Bhugtiar**, aged 14

Chapter Eleven

THE INTERNATIONAL PICTURE

We cannot take it any longer. It is our parents who have let things go on far too long without doing anything. They have failed. We have been forced to fight to the bitter end. **Soweto student**

Go to work and disregard the groups of young intimidators telling people not to go to work. People must go to work and just thrash the children stopping them. **Colonel Visser**, head of South African C.I.D.

Internationally school students have made history, from the Cultural Revolution in China to the demonstrations in South Africa, from children in Zimbabwe joining the guerilla movement of the Patriotic Front to children in Nicaragua and El Salvador joining the same struggle for freedom.

In Denmark children of eight years of age recently initiated a children's rights movement and gained the support of adults. In the USA in 1965 three school children wore black armbands to their respective junior and senior high schools in Des Moines, Iowa, to mourn those who died in the Vietnam War and to support an extension of the Christmas truce. The students were suspended from school for this symbolic act and with the help of the Civil Liberties Union fought the case to the United States Supreme Court. Four years later the Supreme Court handed down an opinion in support of the rights of students (and teachers) to free speech and dissent.

In 1968 French students initiated a movement which nearly

toppled the government. Action Committees were set up in schools to organise the protest:

> "Let us not return to the past. In 1789 there was the abolition of the divine right of kings, in 1936 the divine right of the bosses, and in 1968 we must work to end the divine right of teachers." **Octave Gerard School Action Committee**

> "The schools must no longer be apart from active life, but they must be places where all - workers, peasants, white-collar workers, young and old - will be able to meet, discuss and create together outside school hours." **Hoche Mendon School Action Committee**

> "The administration of the school must be democratic. The Administrative Committee will represent all equally and include: specialised administrators, nominated by the Minister, elected representatives of the teachers, elected representatives of the pupils, elected representatives of the parents." **Buffon School Action Committee**

> "In order to render the role of the teacher more human it is desired that the platform on which he sits be abolished." **Bordeaux School Action Committee**

'Watch out! the students are coming . . .'

In South Africa in 1976 demonstrations and strikes took place all over the country. They were sparked off by the issue of teaching certain school subjects in Afrikaans. School students led the struggle which developed into an attack on the whole racist social system. In a document entitled *A Statement by African High School Pupils*, they describe the situation:

> The main reason for doing all this boycotting of classes, demonstrations and rioting is that we feel we have at last reached the saturation point. To other people, the burning of schools may seem an unreasonable thing to be done by students. We think frustration is the cause of the whole thing.
>
> These so-called anti-riot squads have killed many black people and buried them at night without us knowing. Many of our Black brothers and sisters are shot at night and buried in sacks at night.
>
> These are our immediate demands:
> *We want our fellow students who have been detained to be released
> *Equal jobs
> *Equal pay
> *Free education
> We will never attend classes unless these demands are fulfilled and the South African Government will experience daily rioting if the above-mentioned demands are not fulfilled.

In 1984 South African children led further demonstrations, staging widespread school boycotts. These reached a peak during the newly introduced Coloured and Indian elections when well over 500,000 stayed away from class.

Similarly in 1985, with Apartheid reeling, schools ground to a virtual halt in the black townships. The South African Government formally closed more than 450 mixed-race schools in the Western Cape and 10 black schools near Pretoria because of the spreading unrest.

Pupils were particularly angry at the banning of the Congress of South African Students. Following a school boycott in the black township of Kutlwanong, over the lack of sports facilities and other issues, twenty-five young people aged between fourteen and twenty-five were arrested on 2 May 1985. They were all believed to be members of COSAS. **Sipho Mutsi**, aged eighteen and an

Vietnam War: two girls, aged 17 and 14, after capture by US paratroopers in a guerilla training camp

organiser for COSAS, was one of those arrested. Three days later he died in police custody. According to police he suffered convulsions and fell to the floor while being questioned. But a post mortem revealed a brain haemorrhage and other injuries.

During the year teachers in Soweto faced empty classes for months. **Hamilton Dlamlenae**, secretary-general of the African Teachers' Association of South Africa, said:

> Children are congregating outside the schools and are refusing to go inside. If they do go inside then they refuse to do anything. They just sit there.

In Cape Town a nursery playground group was heard singing 'isibuhlo inja' - 'the bosses are dogs', and other freedom songs.

The South African regime has imprisoned thousands of children precisely because of their prominent role as initiators of resistance. In 1986 children were being detained at the rate of two hundred and fifty a week and, in the last six months of that year, of the twenty-four thousand people detained 40% were under eighteen.

Foreground: *children anticipate the end of apartheid.*
Background: *the state doesn't agree . . .*

In February 1985 nine school students from Gorzow Wielkopolski High School No.1 in Poland were arrested on charges of editing a secret school paper *Sokol* and producing other pamphlets. They were also active in an independent association of high school students. Eight were expelled from school and the six imprisoned were beaten and subjected to repeated interrogation of twelve hours' duration.

In the Reytan school in Warsaw the students spent all recreation periods sitting crouched under the walls as a sign of protest against the arrest of two of their teachers. In one school in Poznan lessons were suspended for a time because students regularly protested by marching in a disciplined file round the playground. In Warsaw and Krakow important anniversaries like the 10th of November - the registration of Solidarity - were marked by the wearing of black.

Two secondary school girls from Kosovo province in Yugoslavia, **Safet Krasniqi** and **Zaja Shala**, are now serving three-year prison sentences for distributing leaflets demanding that Kosovo become a republic within the Socialist Federal Republic of Yugoslavia.

Maria Gorete Joaquim was seventeen when she 'disappeared' in 1979. She was first detained after the invasion of East Timor by Indonesia in 1975 because she was associated with the FRETILIN student organization, Uniao do Estudiante de Timor. It is feared she is dead, executed by her captors.

Gladys Robles Huarocc, aged fourteen, and **Lude Medina Rodriguez**, aged fifteen, used to live in what is now a military zone around the city of Ayacucho in Peru. Since the military command was established in the area over one thousand people have 'disappeared' after being detained by the army. Gladys and Lude were among the nine people rounded up by troops during a raid on their village at 5am on 16 July 1984. They have not been seen since. The authorities will not acknowledge their arrest.   Some of those who have 'disappeared' in Peru were very young. **Gilberto Acuna Chihua** was just ten years old when he 'disappeared' in August 1984. Amnesty International knows of at least eighty-two children and young people under the age of eighteen - minors under Peruvian law - who have 'disappeared' since January 1983. In December 1983, the bodies of six teenagers - three boys and three girls aged between fourteen and eighteen - were found ten miles outside the city of Ayacucho. Their bodies showed signs of torture.

In Corinto, El Salvador, **Evangeline Cabrera**, aged nineteen, was arrested by government troops in January 1985 apparently because she wasn't able to produce her identity papers. Her body has been found. She had been tortured, raped and shot.

In 1986 school children in Haiti went on strike and joined demonstrations against 'Baby Doc' **Duvalier.** Several of them were killed before the movement successfully ousted the dictator.

Chapter Twelve

CONCLUSION

Power to the Imagination. **French Students** , May 1968

Abstinence sows sand all over
The ruddy limbs and flaming hair
But Desire Gratified
Plants fruit of life and beauty there. **William Blake**

T he myth of gentle Jesus meek and mild, which we started with,
has clearly been challenged, as have the notions of 'childish'
and 'childlike', which have come to represent the nature of
childhood. Children are not necessarily immature, nor innocent.
Yet it will take more than a challenge on an ideological level, such
as this book, to make any changes in children's real lives.

In politics children are hardly discussed at all except as they are
part of the family or as they go to school, and these two institutions
are rarely questioned. In fact, the opposite is the case – the main
drift of most political strategies is to strengthen the family and the
school in their control over children. Even when children leave
school there is a desperate attempt now to fit them into one of the
ever-increasing range of training schemes, because there is so little
real work available.

In this age of Star Wars and Chernobyl, adults have little right to
moral authority, as Brecht points out:

It only remains for me, who have so wasted
My life, to beg you
Heed no orders that
Issue from our rotten mouths and
Accept no advice from those who
Have failed so badly, but
Determine for youselves what
Is good for you and what will
Help you cultivate the land that we let go to ruin and
Help to make inhabitable
The cities which we polluted
   Bertolt Brecht, *The Dying Poet's Address to Young People*

121

The recent debate on child abuse has led to a number of educational programmes for children. Their aim is to teach children that their bodies are their own and that they can say no. Yet the irony seems lost on many people that children are hardly encouraged to say no in any other circumstance (or yes, for that matter!). They are not meant to take power over their own lives. The fact that many people still believe in corporal punishment indicates that for them the physical abuse of children is acceptable.

Marge Piercy, in her novel *Woman on the Edge of Time*, describes a society in which sixteen year olds take part in the government, nine and ten year olds do productive labour, and six and seven year olds have sex together.

It is difficult for us to imagine a society in which children play a full part in the activities of that society . How could they be involved in work without being exploited? How could they help create our culture? Why should they not be sexually active? In what ways could their political activities be acknowledged? How could families and schools be transformed? Can we even imagine these things?

Bibliographies

This is a list of books which cover some of the main issues discussed in this book. I have selected mainly recent books, most of which are in print, and ones which are written in reasonably accessible language.

ALTARF – **Challenging Racism**, 1984
>   A collection of articles produced by All London Teachers Against Racism and Fascism showing how school students and teachers can develop effective strategies that challenge racism in schools and in the community.

Judith Ennew – **The Sexual Exploitation of Children**, Polity Press 1986
>   Child sexual exploitation viewed in the broader social context of power relations between men and women, young and old, between classes and between races.

Susan Hemmings (ed.) – **Girls Are Powerful**, Sheba 1982
>   A collection of powerful pieces from *Spare Rib* and *Shocking Pink*, written by young women from seven to twenty-two.

John Holt – **Escape from Childhood**, Penguin 1975
>   Libertarian case for the rights of young children, including the vote, financial independence and the right to choose their guardians.

Stephen Humphries – **Hooligans or Rebels?**, Blackwell 1981
>   An oral history of working-class childhood and youth between 1889 and 1939.

Stevi Jackson – **Childhood and Sexuality**, Blackwell 1982
>   A sensitive discussion of children's sexuality from a feminist perspective with constructive suggestions about how not to hinder its development.

Michael King (ed.) – **Childhood, Welfare and Justice**, Batsford 1981
>   A critical examination of children in the legal and childcare systems, including an essay by Pat Thane on childhood in history.

Jenny Kitteringham – **Country Girls in Nineteenth Century England**, History Workshop 1973
>   A detailed account of girl's work on the farm and in rural industries in the nineteenth century.

London Gay Teenage Group – **Something To Tell You**, 1984
>   Result of a year's research into the lives of 400 young lesbians and gay men in London, containing positive recommendations on employment, the youth service, education, social facilities, resources.

London Gay Teenage Group — **Talking About Young Lesbians**, 1984
Young lesbians talk about their parents, experiences at school, their
sexuality, relationships, men, religion, children, feminism, coming out
and many other aspects of their lives.

Pat Mahony — **Schools for the Boys?**, Hutchinson 1985
Reassesses co-education and deals with sexual harassment. Also
theoretical chapter on the debate around capitalism and patriarchy.

Dave Marsden — **Children's Strikes in 1911**, History Workshop 1973
A docker researching the Hull Dock Strike of 1911 discovers the
nationwide school children's strikes in the same year.

Margaret Mead — **Growing Up in New Guinea**, Penguin 1942
Classic anthropological study of a different kind of childhood.

Roger Mills — **A Comprehensive Education**, Centreprise 1978
A boy's own account of his schooling in East London. He missed
the first week of school and for ever after wondered whether he had
missed the vital explanation that would have made sense of the next
five years!

Dora Russell — **The Tamarisk Tree 2**, Virago 1980
About Beacon Hill School, founded by the Russells in 1927, which
Dora ran on her own between 1932 and 1943. Contemporary with A.S.
Neill's Summerhill.

Dale Spender and Elizabeth Sarah (eds) — **Learning to Lose**, The Women's
Press 1980
Accessible and wide-ranging series of essays on sexism and education.

Striking Miners' Children — **More Valuable Than Gold**, Hoyles 1985
Poetry, prose and drawings showing the political involvement of
miners' children during the 1984/85 strike. Published in Japanese in
1987. (Available from 10 West Bank, London N16 5DG. Cheques for
£2, which includes postage, should be made out to 'More Valuable
Than Gold'. All proceeds to Women Against Pit Closures.)

Valerie Polaskow Suransky — **The Erosion of Childhood**, University of
Chicago Press 1982
How can child care be structured to protect both the interests of children
and the rights of women? Detailed observation and analysis of
American pre-schools and day care centres.

James Walvin — **A Child's World**, Penguin 1982
A social history of English childhood between 1800 and 1914 when
more than a third of the English population was fourteen or under.

Colin Ward — **The Child in the City**, Penguin 1979
An acute commentary on childhood and the urban environment, richly
illustrated with photographs.

Betka Zamoyska — **The Burston Rebellion**, BBC 1985
The book to accompany the brilliant television play about the Burston
school strike.

BIBLIOGRAPHY OF GAY AND LESBIAN BOOKS

This is a selection from the growing number of books now available, particularly from the following bookshops:
Sisterwrite, 190 Upper St, London N1 Tel: 01 226 9782 **Silver Moon**, 68 Charing Cross Rd, London WC2 Tel: 01 836 7906 **Gay's the Word**, 66 Marchmont St, London WC1 Tel: 01 278 7654 **West & Wilde**, 25a Dundas St, Edinburgh EH3 6QQ Tel: 031 556 0079

Most of them should be in print and they are mainly suitable for teenagers. There are only a few suitable for younger children, for example: **When Megan Went Away** by Jane Severance, Lollipop Power, 1979; **Jenny Lives With Eric and Martin** by Susanne Bosche, Gay Men's Press 1983; **Your Family, My Family** by Joan Drescher, Walker 1980

The best reference books on the subject are Barbara Grier's **The Lesbian in Literature**, Naiad 1981, which is a comprehensive annotated bibliography of 3,000 books, and Ian Young's **The Male Homosexual in Literature**, Scarecrow Press 1982, which contains 4,000 titles.

LESBIAN FICTION

Sarah Aldridge – **All True Lovers**, Naiad 1978
Rita Mae Brown – **Rubyfruit Jungle**, Corgi 1978
Michelle Cliff – **Abeng**, The Crossing Press 1984
Nancy Garden – **Annie On My Mind**, Farrar, Straus & Giroux 1982
Rosa Guy – **Ruby**, Viking 1976
Deborah Hautzig – **Hey, Dollface**, Fontana 1978
Lee Lynch – **Toothpick House**, Naiad 1983
Elizabeth A. Lynn – **Watchtower**, Berkley 1979
Elizabeth A Lynn – **The Dancers of Arun**, Berkley 1979
Elizabeth A. Lynn – **The Northern Girl**, Berkley 1980
Rosemary Manning – **The Chinese Garden**, Brilliance Books 1984
Isabel Miller – **Patience and Sarah**, The Women's Press 1979
Victoria Ramstetter – **The Marquise and the Novice**, Naiad 1983
Mary Renault – **The Charioteer**, New English Library 1968
Jane Rule – **Desert of the Heart**, Naiad 1983
Sandra Scoppettone – **Happy Endings Are All Alike**, Dell 1978
Sandra Scoppettone – **Trying Hard To Hear You**, Harper & Row 1974
Alice Walker – **The Colour Purple**, The Women's Press 1983
Jeanette Winterson – **Oranges Are Not The Only Fruit**, Pandora 1985

GAY FICTION

B.A. Ecker — **Independence Day**, Avon/Flare 1983
Jeffrey M. Elliot (ed.) — **Kindred Spirits, An Anthology of Gay and Lesbian Science Fiction Stories**, Alyson 1984
E.M. Forster — **Maurice**, Penguin 1972
Lynn Hall — **Sticks and Stones**, Follett 1977
Emily Hanlon — **The Wing and the Flame**, Bantam 1983
Laura Z. Hobson — **Consenting Adult**, Warner 1976
Timothy Ireland — **Who Lies Inside**, Gay Men's Press 1984
Clay Larkin — **A Different Love**, Alyson 1983
Frank Mosca — **All-American Boys**, Alyson 1983
David Rees — **In the Tent**, Dobson 1979
David Rees — **Quintin's Man**, Dobson 1976
David Rees — **The Estuary**, Gay Men's Press 1983
David Rees — **The Milkman's On His Way**, Gay Men's Press 1982
Anne Snyder — **Counter Play**, New American Library 1981
Edmund White — **A Boy's Own Story**, Picador 1983

NON-FICTION

Sidney Abbot & Barbara Love — **Sappho Was A Right-On Woman**, Stein & Day 1972
Nancy Adair & Casey Adair — **Word Is Out**, Dell 1978
Sasha Alyson — **Young, Gay and Proud**, Alyson 1980
Jack Babuscio — **We Speak for Ourselves**, SPCK
Chris Beer, Roland Jeffery & Terry Munyard — **Gay Workers**, NCCL 1981
Ruth Bell — **Changing Bodies, Changing Lives**, Random House 1980
Vern L. Bullough — **Homosexuality: A History**, New American Library 1979
Jane Cousins — **Make It Happy**, Virago 1978
Paul Crane — **Gays and the Law**, Pluto 1982
Margaret Cruikshank (ed.) — **The Lesbian Path**, Naiad 1981
Liz Diamond — **The Lesbian Primer**, Women's Educational Media 1979
Betty Fairchild & Nancy Hayward — **Now That You Know**, Harcourt Brace Jovanovich 1979
Aaron Fricke — **Reflections of a Rock Lobster**, Alyson 1981
Bruce Galloway — **A Campaign Manual for Gay People**, Grass Roots 1982
Bruce Galloway (ed.) — **Prejudice and Pride**, Routledge & Kegan Paul 1983
Gay Teachers Group & Socialist Teachers Alliance — **School's Out**, London Gay Teacher's Group 1983
Gemma — **Disabled Gays Guide**, Gemma 1983/4
Frances Hanckel & John Cunningham — **A Way of Love, A Way of Life: A Young Person's Introduction to What It Means To Be Gay**, Lothrop, Lee & Shepard 1979
John Hart — **So You Think You're Attracted To The Same Sex?**, Penguin 1984
Heinz Heger — **The Men With The Pink Triangle**, Gay Men's Press 1980
Ann Heron (ed.) **One Teenager in Ten**, Alyson 1983

Joint Council for Gay Teenagers — **I Know What I Am**, JCTG 1980
Joint Council for Gay Teenagers — **Breaking the Silence**, JCTG
John Lauritsen & David Thorstad — **The Early Homosexual Rights Movement (1864-1935)**, Times Change Press 1974
London Gay Teenage Group — **Talking About School**, LGTG 1984
Del Martin & Phyllis Lyon — **Lesbian Woman**, Bantam 1972
Julia Penelope Stanley & Susan Wolfe (eds.) — **The Coming Out Stories**, Persephone Press 1980
Ginny Vida (ed.) — **Our Right To Love, A Lesbian Resource Book**, National Gay Task Force 1978
George Weinberg — **Society and the Healthy Homosexual**, Colin Smythe 1972
Youth Liberation — **Growing Up Gay**, Youth Liberation Press 1978

CREDITS

Pp29, 105: *The English at Home*, Bill Brandt, Batsford 1936; pp52, 53: *Something to tell you*, Lorraine Trenchard and Hugh Warren, London Gay Teenage Group 1984; p60: photo by Sally and Richard Greenhill 1984; p73: photo by Ian Steel; p107: *The Encyclopaedia of Horror*, David Carson, Hamlyn 1981; p108: *Jenny Lives with Eric and Martin*, Gay Men's Press 1983; p109 *Newark Advertiser*.